Landmarks of world literature

Gottfried von Strassburg

TRISTAN

GOTTFRIED VON STRASSBURG

Tristan

MARK CHINCA
University of Cambridge

831.6
G 713c

CAMBRIDGE
UNIVERSITY PRESS

Published by the Press Syndicate of the University of Cambridge
The Pitt Building Trumpington Street, Cambridge CB2 1RP
40 West 20th Street, New York, NY 10011-4211, USA
10 Stamford Road, Oakleigh, Melbourne 3166, Australia

First published 1997

Printed in Great Britain at the University Press, Cambridge

A catalogue record for this book is available from the British Library

Library of Congress cataloguing in publication data

Chinca, Mark.
Gottfried von Strassburg, Tristan/Mark Chinca.
    p.   cm. – (Landmarks of world literature)
Includes bibliographical references.
ISBN 0 521 40294 8. – ISBN 0 521 40852 0 (paperback)
1. Gottfried, von Strassburg, 13th cent. Tristan.   2. Tristan
(Legendary character) – Romances – History and criticism.
3. Arthurian romances – History and criticism.   I. Title.
II. Series.
PT1526.C47   1997
831'.6 – dc20   96–24762   CIP

ISBN 0521 40294 8 hardback
ISBN 0521 40852 0 paperback

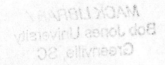

AAS-5887

Contents

Acknowledgments

My thanks are due to the many people who helped me to write this book, sometimes without knowing it: to students who asked questions, to colleagues who answered my own, and above all to Dennis Green, who followed the project from inception to completion, read every draft of every chapter, and never failed to provide just the encouragement I needed.

Note on the text

The names of the story's main characters have variant forms and spellings in the medieval sources. I have retained some of the peculiarities (for instance 'Tristran' in the case of the French romances), but normalized and also anglicized a little, so that readers will not be disconcerted by outlandish spellings ('Marke', 'Isôt') on which it would be pedantic to insist. The forms 'Tristan', 'Isolde', 'Mark' are used for Gottfried's protagonists, and wherever these characters are mentioned without reference to a particular work.

Gottfried is quoted from the edition by Friedrich Ranke, *Tristan und Isold*, fifteenth edition, Dublin and Zurich, 1978; line-numbers also refer to this edition. Where the first reference to other primary sources or to secondary literature appears as a short title, full details will be found in the 'Guide to further reading' at the end of this book. References to the *Patrologia Latina* and the *Monumenta Germaniae Historica* are given as *PL* or *MGH* followed by the volume and column or page number.

The translations of Gottfried (and of most other primary sources) are my own. This does not imply negative judgment of A. T. Hatto's excellent translation of *Tristan* for the Penguin Classics; it simply suited my purpose sometimes to have a more literal rendering than Hatto gives, or one that emphasized a different nuance of meaning in the original.

Introduction

'O everlasting night, sweet night, sacred, exalted night of love! He who has felt your embrace and your smile, how could he ever awake from you without pangs of dread?' Thus sing Wagner's lovers Tristan and Isolde. Their 'Liebesnacht', the night of love, becomes the 'Liebestod' in the continuation of their duet: 'Banish now those pangs, gentle death, love-death of our ardent longing! In your arms, consecrated to you, hallowed warmth of ages, we are free from awaking's duress!' (*Tristan und Isolde*, ed. W. Zentner, Stuttgart, 1950, act II, scene 2). Night and death are the fulfilment of love. Nothing could be further from the medieval source on which Wagner freely based his story-line, the Middle High German verse romance *Tristan*, written around 1210 by Gottfried von Strassburg; nor is it anything like the source that Gottfried used, the Old French *Roman de Tristan* by Thomas. In the medieval versions, there is nothing metaphysical about the lovers' death. Thomas leaves them side by side on the bier, summing up tersely, 'Tristran died for his love, and fair Ysolt of a tender heart' (ed. Wind, Sneyd[2], 818–19). The scene is not included in Gottfried's unfinished romance, but he does narrate the death of Tristan's parents, Riwalin and Blanscheflur. The father dies, not for love, but in a feudal war he incautiously provoked with his neighbour; the mother does not survive her grief. This is no 'Liebestod': there is no mystical togetherness, no ecstatic abandon, no hint that in death love triumphs over time and adversity.

There is a time and place in Gottfried where love endures. It is not a metaphysical realm of death, but very much in this life. It is the time and place of Gottfried's own writing. The love of Tristan and Isolde lives for as long as it is commemorated in literature. Gottfried puts it thus near the end of the prologue with which he introduces the story: 'Although the lovers are

1

long dead, yet their sweet name lives' (ed. Ranke, 222–3). The idea that writing preserves the glory of the past from oblivion is commonplace in classical and medieval historiography; Gottfried goes further, however, by suggesting that not only is the dead lovers' memory kept alive by literature, death itself is undone: 'For wherever their loyalty, their loyal purity, their hearts' joy and their hearts' sorrow are still read out to us, it is bread for all noble hearts. With this their death lives' (230–4). The story has life-giving, transformative power; in the medium of the literary word, whenever and wherever it is told and heard, the dead come to life. Gottfried's claim for the power of his fiction is prodigious, and the brilliance with which he makes good that claim establishes his work as a landmark in European writing.

Chapter 1

Story, author, context

The story

(1) Gottfried's narrative begins with Tristan's parents, Riwalin, the lord of Parmenie, and Blanscheflur, the sister of King Mark of Cornwall. They fall in love while Riwalin is perfecting his chivalry at Mark's court; she becomes pregnant and elopes with him to Parmenie, where they marry. Riwalin is killed in a war with his old enemy Duke Morgan; grief-stricken, Blanscheflur gives birth to a son and dies. (245–1790)

(2) The orphan is adopted by Riwalin's marshal, Rual, and his wife Floraete. In order to protect Riwalin's heir from Morgan's violence, they give out that the child is their own; they baptize him Tristan. The boy receives training in all the accomplishments that make the perfect knight and courtier. Fourteen years old, he is kidnapped by Norwegian merchants and eventually released in Cornwall. Thanks to his skills as huntsman, musician and linguist, he wins the favour of King Mark and his court, pretending all the while to be the son of a merchant from Parmenie. The pretence ends when Rual, who has been searching for his foster-son for over three years, turns up in Cornwall and reveals to Mark and Tristan that they are uncle and nephew. The king accepts Tristan as legitimate kin, and dubs him a knight. (1791–5068)

(3) Tristan goes home to Parmenie as Riwalin's successor. He enfeoffs his vassals, avenges his father's death by killing Morgan, and knights Rual's sons along with several others, including his tutor and loyal friend Curvenal. Then he hands over his territory to Rual and his sons, and returns to Mark, who has already declared that his nephew will succeed him.

Tristan kills the giant Morold, who has come to exact the tribute regularly paid by Cornwall to Ireland, in a judicial combat; a splinter of Tristan's sword remains lodged in Morold, who deals Tristan a poisonous wound which nobody can cure except his sister, the Irish queen Isolde. Tristan voyages to Ireland, disguised as the minstrel-cum-merchant 'Tantris'; his musicianship wins him an audience with the queen, who heals him in exchange for teaching her daughter, also called Isolde. Not long after his return from Ireland, the Cornish barons urge Mark to marry and produce a direct heir. Their motive is jealousy of Tristan. Mark insists that he will marry only Princess Isolde, thinking that the enmity between Cornwall and Ireland rules out all chance of obtaining her hand. Tristan volunteers to lead the wooing-expedition, and voyages to Ireland for the second time, disguised once more as Tantris. He slays a dragon, the feat of prowess nearly costing him his life. He is nursed by Queen Isolde and her daughter, who notices one day that the splinter recovered from her dead uncle Morold's head fits the gap in Tantris' sword. Thus Tristan's identity is discovered, but his life is spared, because he must be produced as a witness against the steward, who has been claiming that he killed the dragon and consequently is entitled to the hand of Princess Isolde in reward. After the steward has been exposed as a fraud, the Irish king Gurmun confirms the settlement already agreed with Tristan: he will make peace with Cornwall, and give his daughter to Mark in marriage. Tristan brings Isolde back to Cornwall. On board ship they accidentally drink a love-potion prepared by the queen for her daughter and Mark. (5069–12411)

(4) As the ships approach Cornwall, the lovers fear the consequences of Mark's discovering that his bride is not a virgin. Isolde persuades her companion Brangaene to take her place in bed on the wedding-night. The deception is successful, yet Isolde is afraid that her secret is not safe with Brangaene. She hires killers, but Brangaene gives proof of her loyalty and discretion. An Irish baron, Gandin, tricks Mark into giving Isolde to him, only to be tricked himself by Tristan, who wins

her back for Mark. There follows a series of intrigues, in which the same basic scenario is repeated: the king's suspicion is aroused, he tries to obtain proof by means of a ruse, but thanks to the superior cunning of the lovers ends up convinced of their innocence. First, Mark tries to catch Isolde out during his bed-time conversations with her, but she persuades him that she detests Tristan. Then he spies on one of the lovers' assignations in the orchard; they realize the danger and put on a show of innocence. Finally, flour is strewn between the lovers' beds. It shows no trace of their coming and going, but there is blood on the sheets, from a wound of Tristan's which broke open when, perceiving the trap, he jumped from his bed into Isolde's and back. Perplexed by these conflicting indices, Mark requires Isolde to clear her name by swearing an oath on a hot iron. She triumphs in the ordeal, swearing that no man has lain by her except her husband, and a pilgrim who stumbled to the ground with her as he carried her ashore to take her oath. The pilgrim is Tristan in disguise. (12412–15764)

(5) Tristan leaves the scene of the ordeal for South Wales. As a reward for killing a giant he receives a magical dog, Petitcriu, whose bell banishes cares. He sends the dog to Isolde; she removes its bell, so that she can be in sadness, like her lover. (15765–16402)

(6) Tristan is back at court. Mark's suspicions are rekindled, this time by the lovers' demeanour; unable to bear it, he banishes them. (16403–678)

(7) The lovers withdraw to a cave, set in an idyllic landscape. They have a perfect life, until one day the royal hunt passes nearby. The lovers take precautions; Mark discovers them asleep on either side of a sword, and is convinced once more of their innocence. (16679–17658)

(8) Mark allows the lovers to return to court, but forbids any intimacy. He finds them together in bed in the orchard, but by the time he has fetched witnesses, Tristan has departed. (17659–18404)

(9) Tristan flees abroad, and distinguishes himself in military service, in particular with Duke Jovelin of Arundel (which Gottfried locates on the continent). An attachment develops between Tristan and the duke's daughter, whose name, Isolde Whitehand, reminds him of his first love. (18405–19548)

The work breaks off here because, we are told by authors who continued it later in the thirteenth century, Gottfried died before he could finish it. The continuations are discussed in the conclusion to this book; the remainder of the plot can be reconstructed from Gottfried's source, Thomas, and other related versions. Tristan marries Isolde Whitehand, but does not sleep with his wife out of loyalty to the first Isolde, whose statue he adores in secret. He takes his brother-in-law Kaedin into his confidence; in disguise, they twice return to Cornwall to see Isolde. Back in Arundel, Tristan is lethally wounded by a poisoned lance when he rescues the mistress of a fellow lover, Dwarf Tristan, from a giant. Kaedin is dispatched to fetch Isolde to cure him; his ship is to have a white sail if the mission has been successful, black if not. Isolde Whitehand overhears this and, as the ship approaches, falsely tells her husband that its sail is black. Tristan turns to the wall and dies. Isolde lands too late to help, lies down beside him and dies.

The author

We know nothing about Gottfried as an historical person except his name and that he died without completing *Tristan*; this work, along with two short poems on the themes of covetousness and fortune, are all we have of him.

Authors of medieval romances usually name themselves in a prologue, but Gottfried does not, or in an epilogue, which *Tristan*, being unfinished, does not have. Gottfried does, however, reveal part of his name in another way. The manuscripts of *Tristan* follow the common practice of marking sections of text by an enlarged initial; in the sequence of these initials it is possible to discern an acrostic made up of the entwined names Gottfried, Dietrich, Tristan and Isolde:

```
G  DIETERICH  TIIT  O  RSSR  T  IOOI  E  SLLS  (F  TDDT  R  AEEA  I  NNNN  T)

G              O      T       E       (F    R      I           T)
   DIETERICH

            T      R      I      S      (T       A      N)
            I      S      O      L      (D       E      N)
            I      S      O      L      (D       E      N)
            T      R      I      S      (T       A      N)
```

The letters in brackets show how the acrostic would have
continued if the text had been finished. *Isolden* is an oblique case
form of the heroine's name, assumed in order to make the
acrostic work out neatly (the forms used by Gottfried in the text
are *Isôt*, *Isolt*, nominative, *Isôte*, *Isolde*, oblique). The identification of *Dieterich* is uncertain; most probably this is the name
of Gottfried's patron and dedicatee of the work. If so, then the
acrostic interweaves all the primary elements of literary
communication, author, story (represented by its main characters)
and audience (represented by the work's most important
addressee).

Gottfried's full name is known to us only from later authors
who call him 'meister Gotfrit von Strazburc'. The title *meister*
expresses their admiration of his artistic mastery; additionally
it may be a specific designation of social class (a burgher, as
opposed to a noble *hêr*) or educational status (*magister artium*,
a graduate who had mastered the traditional curriculum of the
seven liberal arts). It is impossible to be certain about Gottfried's
social status or how relevant it is to understanding *Tristan*; on
the other hand, the work is unmistakably that of an author
keen to demonstrate his learning. Gottfried was what contemporary Latin writers called a *clericus* and a *litteratus*; the terms
do not mean exactly the same thing as 'cleric' and 'literate', but
denote in Gottfried's case someone with academic education
and familiarity with Latin. Only mastery of the *trivium* (the
three arts of grammar, rhetoric and dialectic) can explain
Gottfried's acquaintance with classical literature, his elegant
style and his skill in presenting arguments; his informed

comments on music suggest study of the *quadrivium* (music, astronomy, arithmetic and geometry). Beyond the seven liberal arts lie the higher academic disciplines of law, philosophy and theology; these too have left their mark on Gottfried's work. The terminology in the story's many judicial scenes is exact, and the whole work owes much of its seductive allusiveness to the author's ability to exploit the resonances of philosophical and theological language.

It is possible that, like many Germans of his generation, Gottfried studied in France, whose schools nurtured the most advanced intellectual culture in Europe. He certainly seems knowledgeable about French intellectual life, and mentions by name two leading centres for music, Sens and St-Denis, when describing the 'French style' of Isolde's playing (8061–2). It would also explain how he acquired the competence in French needed to work with his source, Thomas.

The date of *Tristan*

Tristan is thought to have been written around 1210. There is no external evidence for this date; it is the best conjecture we can make on the basis of what we presume to be textual allusions to contemporary persons, events and controversies.

(1) In the narrative of Tristan's accolade Gottfried embeds a literary excursus in which he singles out for praise or censure a number of other authors. One writer, whom Gottfried does not name but refers to as 'the companion of the hare' (4638), is criticized for his obscurity. Gottfried probably means Wolfram von Eschenbach and his Grail romance *Parzival*; its style is notoriously difficult, and in the prologue Wolfram declares that his opening metaphor eludes the slow-witted like a hare startled by the huntsman's bell (ed. E. Nellmann, Frankfurt, 1994, 1,15–19). The composition of *Parzival* can be dated with some likelihood to the decade 1200–10, from which it follows that Gottfried must also have been writing around that time.

(2) Isolde's exculpation by ordeal is said by Gottfried to show 'that Christ the miracle-worker is like a sleeve which takes its shape according to the wind; where one knows how to petition him right, he bends and clings as pliantly and closely as by rights he should' (15735–40). These words must be understood as criticism of trial by ordeal, the judicial practice of establishing a person's guilt by a physical test, such as holding hot iron. It was believed that God revealed the truth in the outcome. Gottfried's simile (one must picture an ample sleeve, with loose material hanging down, as in ecclesiastical vestments) is an ironic comment on this belief: Isolde's successful avoidance of detection by means of a cleverly worded oath demonstrates that ordeals merely cloak human manipulation with a semblance of divine judgment. The objection was not new. In 1098 William Rufus, hearing that fifty men charged with taking his deer had been proved innocent by ordeal, angrily declared, 'From now on answer shall be made to my judgment, not to God's, which can be bent ('plicatur'; cf. Gottfried's 'vüegen') to either side by each man's prayer'. Eadmer, the church historian who reported this remark, viewed the king's scepticism as a sign of irreligious pride (*Historia Novorum in Anglia*, ed. M. Rule, London, 1884, p. 102); yet from the late eleventh century it was largely churchmen – theologians and canon lawyers – who voiced cogent and continuous opposition to trial by ordeal. They denounced it as manipulable, as lacking biblical and legal authority, and as blasphemous temptation of God. The campaign achieved its goal under the reforming papacy of Innocent III (1198–1216); at the fourth Lateran council in 1215, the church prohibited the involvement of priests in administering ordeals. In the years leading up to this decision, which resulted in the procedure's abolition, the objections were rehearsed with particular energy; their echo in Gottfried's mocking and ironic comment is conveniently explained if we suppose him to be writing at that time.

The arguments against trial by ordeal were certainly in the air of early thirteenth-century Strassburg. The bishop, Heinrich II von Veringen, considered ordeals an appropriate procedure in cases of heresy; for this he was admonished by the pope, who in a letter dated 9 January 1212 pointed out that ordeals were not allowed by the church, because of the biblical injunction 'You shall not tempt the Lord your God' (*PL* 216, 502). In the same year eighty or more men and women were charged with heresy at Strassburg and required to undergo the ordeal of the hot iron; most were convicted and executed (*MGH Scriptores*, 17, p. 174). By remarking ironically on Isolde's ordeal, Gottfried could have been using this traditional episode of the Tristan story as a vehicle for attacking his bishop's policy at a time when the pope himself was denouncing it.

Strassburg

The city in which Gottfried wrote for his original public was a thriving commercial centre with a population of around 10,000. It had a history of factional strife, between the bishops who traditionally ruled Strassburg and the leading citizens whose growing wealth encouraged them to demand political and legal independence. The civil war that broke out in Germany in 1198 between rival claimants to the throne provided the citizens with an opportunity. When Philip of Swabia took Strassburg in 1205, their support was rewarded with a new constitution which conferred the status of free imperial city (the bishop was on the side of Philip's opponent, Otto of Brunswick). The settlement was not the end of conflict in the city; episcopal rule was restored in 1214–19, and it was only after a decisive military victory in 1262 that Strassburg was undisputedly governed by its citizens.

It is tempting to look for a direct reflexion of this civic discord in Gottfried's work. The search yields only possibilities which cannot be elevated even to probabilities. Even if Gottfried's attack on ordeals is aimed specifically at the Bishop of Strassburg, this does not necessarily make him a partisan of the citizens; he could, like the pope, be criticizing from a clerical point of view. Similarly, the references to merchants in the work are no reliable indication that Gottfried felt a personal affinity with this class; if this line of reasoning is admitted, then one can equally well argue for Gottfried's pro-episcopal sympathies on the basis of his positive portrayal of the fictional Bishop of Thamise (15425–68). Finally, it does not follow from Gottfried's many ironic and sarcastic comments about chivalry and the court that his work reflects a specifically bourgeois outlook; there is a tradition of court satire by clerics. None of this is to deny that the historical Gottfried von Strassburg may have had political allegiances; it is simply a reminder that his work on its own does not reveal them unambiguously. Nor can one deny that patricians were among Gottfried's public, and that they might have interpreted certain aspects of *Tristan* in a partisan or class-specific way. But this does not necessarily mean that the work was intended exclusively for them; patricians might have been one group only in a heterogeneous audience.

It is interesting that on two separate occasions Gottfried appeals to the courtliness of his public, once when passing over the medical details of Tristan's cure as 'uncourtly talk' (7954), and again when refusing to offer a long discourse on love, which would be tiresome for 'courtly sensibilities' (12183–4). The term 'courtly' is not being used here descriptively, but *rhetorically*: these passages are an invitation to the public to define themselves as courtly people, no matter what their particular class or factional allegiance. From what we can surmise about the literary scene in early thirteenth-century Strassburg, it is likely that the audience for *Tristan* comprised members of the different groups who made up the social and intellectual elite of the city: secular aristocrats and patricians, ministerials (administrators and officials) of the bishop, and clerics. The last group was socially diverse; the senior clergy of the cathedral chapter were drawn predominantly from the local nobility, whereas members of the collegiate foundation of St Thomas and the foundation of Jung-St Peter belonged to patrician families. The category of courtliness could bridge sectional differences within this elite, because it is sociologically vague and connotes distinction on the basis of refined manners and high moral purpose. Anyone, whether or not he is noble by birth, can be courtly in this sense. By appealing to his public's courtliness, Gottfried could foster a common sense of identity among them;

moreover, by insinuating their involvement in courtliness, he could also ensure their interest in its satirization.

German literature around 1200

In his literary excursus Gottfried describes German literature as a tree whose many branches are covered in flowers for him and his contemporaries to pick. The late twelfth and early thirteenth centuries were indeed a 'Blütezeit', a period in which German literature attained an extraordinary florescence. Besides Gottfried, the famous names in courtly romance are Heinrich von Veldeke, Hartmann von Aue and Wolfram von Eschenbach; lyric is represented by Reinmar, Heinrich von Morungen and Walther von der Vogelweide; and no list of great works of the period would be complete without the anonymous heroic epic, the *Nibelungenlied*.

Rather than outline the chronological development of this literature, the following paragraphs give a sketch of its physiognomy. The aim is to highlight the most important features and tendencies which also left their mark on Gottfried's writing. Following Nigel Palmer (*German Literary Culture*, pp. 6–11) we may situate German literature around 1200 in the opposition (and intersection) of three pairs of concepts: written – oral, Latin – vernacular, religious – profane.

(1) *Written – oral*. We take it for granted nowadays that literature is written and read. In Germany at the turn of the thirteenth century members of the social elite (the class for which literature was produced) had until recently belonged to one of two cultures: the oral culture of secular princes, nobles and knights, whose education did not usually involve literacy, and the book-culture of the *clerici* and *litterati*, which was predominantly Latin. The emergence of an independent written literature in German is, therefore, a sign that the two cultures were beginning to intersect. Literacy, whose main centres had been in monasteries and episcopal courts, entered the oral world of secular rulers from the middle of the twelfth century, as chanceries were established at feudal courts and in towns to

deal with the increasingly complex tasks of administration. Chanceries, staffed by literate, educated clerics, did not only meet administrative needs; they provided interested aristocrats and patricians with the capacity for having works of literature written in the vernacular.

The fact that a significant German-language book-culture emerged in the second half of the twelfth century does not necessarily mean that laymen were becoming literate. Only a few of them could read, even when the books were written in German; their reasons for investing in a written literature of their own (a book was a considerable investment, for parchment was costly) often had as much to do with a desire for self-aggrandizement as with intellectual curiosity. Wealthy princes wished to magnify their reputations by exercising the literary patronage that hitherto had been open only to kings, and the world and values of the secular elite as a whole were dignified through being represented in books. Yet these laymen would not have been convinced of the desirability of literature if they had not also some appreciation of the *contents* of books. By their very involvement with written literature, they were no longer pure *illitterati* (the term used by the *litterati* to describe those who did not belong to their culture), but *quasi litterati*, people not actually able to read, but whose attitudes were formed in part by book-culture, to which they had access through hearing the written word read aloud.

Because most of the public for works written in German could not read, and because manuscripts were anyway expensive to produce, literature reached its audience principally by being read out. Those who were restricted to hearing a work in recital will have experienced it differently from the minority who could additionally read it. (The word 'additionally' must be emphasized: readers also were present at recitals, not least because in this pre-print era books were too scarce and precious for everyone to possess his own copy.) Pure listeners may not have heard all of a longer work, just episodes. Not only would readers know the whole story, private reading allowed them the opportunity to reflect on its themes, patterns and meaning.

(2) *Latin – vernacular.* Throughout the Middle Ages Latin enjoyed undisputed prestige as the language of an unbroken tradition of literature and learning stretching back to antiquity. This was the book-culture of the *clerici* and *litterati*. The growth of written literature in German indicates that other groups outside this educational elite, nobles, patricians and knights, were sponsoring their own book-culture, chiefly in the roles of patron and public. The authors, however, of this written literature were largely clerics, like Gottfried, whose standards were those of Latin culture. The influence of Latin can be detected in all written vernacular literature, whether its material is taken from native traditions of oral poetry, like the *Nibelungenlied*, or from books written in French, like *Tristan*. German literature is nevertheless distinct from Latin, and not just because it is in another language. It has its own genres, without parallels in either classical or medieval Latin; as clerical learning is deployed in this different context, it takes on new functions and meanings.

(3) *Religious – profane.* There was literature in German before chanceries brought clerics and their book-culture closer into the world of the feudal and urban elite. This early literature is typically religious in content, written by monks, secular clerics and the occasional pious layman for the edification of those with no Latin. Then, around the middle of the twelfth century, the emphasis changes to include worldly themes, of which the principal ones are love and chivalry. This shift reflects the increasing part that laymen played in determining what was written. Political stability and economic prosperity in the twelfth century gave rise to a secular elite who displayed their new-found cultural confidence in the forms and institutions of chivalry and courtliness: tournaments, festivals, dress, deportment, and literature. This courtly culture was a European phenomenon; its earliest centres are in France and the Low Countries, from where it spread to Germany. The literature was no exception; much of it, including *Tristan*, was adapted from French sources, usually by clerics who could read the manuscripts.

This profane literature, which was cultivated at aristocratic courts and, from around 1200, in the cities, was not free of all religious influence. There are structural interferences, for instance between hagiography and the secular genres of romance and epic, as well as thematic and poetological interferences, the latter occurring when authors describe reading or listening to profane literature in terms borrowed from Christian religion and liturgy. Yet it is not enough merely to register the parallels; as with Latin influence, one must also ask whether and how the religious model has been adapted, or even transformed, as it is transferred from one sphere to another.

The interplay of literacy and orality, Latin and vernacular, religious and profane shapes Gottfried's writing as it shaped all German literature of the period. We shall have to consider how far his writing was directed particularly at the literate (only readers, for instance, can work out the acrostic and appreciate its significance), and in addition to noting his many borrowings from classical and religious sources, we shall have to ask whether and how he adapts what he borrows. But before fixing our attention exclusively on Gottfried's work, we must set it in one more context, that of the medieval Tristan tradition.

Chapter 2

Gottfried and the Tristan tradition

God creates, man imitates. Such were the limits placed on human creativity by Hugh of St Victor (1097–1141), who formulated a hierarchical division of labour between God, nature and man: God alone can make something out of nothing; nature brings forth what was hidden; the human artificer copies nature, joining what was dispersed and separating what was joined (*PL* 176, 747). Hugh gives a theologian's perspective on what in any case was an important characteristic of medieval art and literature, the one that modern observers are also most likely to find disconcerting: its traditionalism. Visual artists reproduced models; lyric poets drew on a common stock of situations, roles, metaphors and genres, reworking and recombining them; narrative authors retold stories about people whose names and exploits were already fixed in the repertoire of tradition. Gottfried, on his own admission, is no exception: 'I know well that there have been many who have told the story of Tristan' (131–2). The tradition not only provided Gottfried with a story, however; it also presented him with different ways of telling it. In order to see which possibilities Gottfried took up and developed, we must approach his work through the tradition out of which it came.

Traditionalism need not mean monotony or lack of originality, in spite of what detractors of medieval literature might say. Of cosmology – a traditional way of accounting for the world and man's place in it – the anthropologist Mary Douglas has written that we should try to think of it 'as a set of categories that are in use [...] not a hard carapace which the tortoise has to carry for ever, but something very flexible and easily disjointed. Spare parts can be fitted and adjustments made without trouble' (*Natural Symbols*, London, 1970, p. 144). The same may be said of medieval literary tradition. It has two aspects, one conservative and guaranteeing continuity with the past, the other dynamic, renewing and updating the past so that it remains relevant to the present. A tradition stays alive thanks to this capacity for renewal. Medieval authors set great store by their role as guardians of tradition, yet they also laid emphasis on doing something new. Wolfram von Eschenbach announces the story of Parzival with the words 'I want to renew ['niuwen'] a story for you; its theme is great loyalty' (ed. E. Nellmann, Frankfurt, 1994, 4,9–10). The verb *niuwen* here can mean 'to tell again' (Wolfram is picking up a story told by his predecessor Chrétien de Troyes) and 'to tell in a new way'. Gottfried states in the prologue to his romance that 'even nowadays it is pleasing for us to hear about the lovers' inmost loyalty, sweet and ever new' ('uns ist noch hiute liep vernomen, / süeze und iemer niuwe / ir inneclichiu triuwe') (218–20). The last two lines could have been inverted without injury to rhyme or sense. Instead, Gottfried has opted for what grammarians call construction *apo koinou*: two phrases (here the first and third lines) have an element in common (the middle line). The adjectives *süeze* and *niuwe* can be seen as qualifying the noun *triuwe*; this interpretation is reflected in the translation. But they can also be construed as qualifiers of the preceding past participle *vernomen*, in apposition to *liep*, giving the meaning 'it is pleasing, sweet and ever new for us to hear'. Through this ambivalent placing of the adjectives, Gottfried associates the idea of renewal with both the act of listening and its object, loyalty. The resulting implication is that through hearing the old story anew the lovers' inmost loyalty is made sweet and new.

The tradition before 1200

We are well placed to observe the interplay of tradition and renewal in the case of Tristan and Isolde. Their love is the theme of a great many texts in verse and prose composed between the twelfth and sixteenth centuries all over Europe, from Scandinavia and the Iberian peninsula to Serbia and Greece. From the 1150s the story was sufficiently well known in French and German literary circles to be the object of allusions in songs by troubadours, trouvères and minnesingers. Bernart de Ventadorn complains that he endures more pain than 'the lover Tristan, who suffered many sorrows of love for fair Isolde' (*Chansons d'amour*, ed. M. Lazar, Paris, 1966, IV, 45–9); Chrétien insists that 'I never drank of the philtre that poisoned Tristan; yet I love more than he thanks to a fine heart and pure will' (*Œuvres complètes*, ed. D. Poirion, Paris, 1994, song II, 28–31); Heinrich von Veldeke also contrasts the involuntary passion of Tristan to his own love: 'Tristan had to be constant to the queen against his will, for he was compelled by the potion more than the force of love. My good lady should thank me, because I never drank any such philtre and yet I love her better than he, if that can be' (*Mittelhochdeutsche Minnelyrik I*, ed. G. Schweikle, Darmstadt, 1977, song IV, 1–4). Familiarity with the whole Tristan story is likewise the background to the *lais*, short narrative poems, which recount a single episode in the lovers' long affair. From the second half of the twelfth century we have *Chevrefoil*, the lay of the honeysuckle, attributed to Marie de France, the two versions of the *Folie Tristan*, and the inset lay of Tristan and Isolde in the *Donnei des amants*. These poems record how, by one means or another, the lovers evade Mark's surveillance in order to be together; they are in other words variations on a scenario repeatedly enacted in the romances: a tryst facilitated by a ruse.

Of the many full-length narratives let us concentrate on the earliest surviving romances in verse, composed in French and German in the second half of the twelfth century, for these are our main evidence of the tradition to which Gottfried added his own voice soon after 1200. A fragment of a Tristan romance, narrating the story from the lovers' assignation overheard by Mark in the orchard to the first stages of the hero's exile, is preserved in a French manuscript of the second half of the thirteenth century. The romance was composed in the twelfth century, perhaps in the 1190s, or possibly earlier, around 1160; nothing is known about the author, Beroul, and there is even a theory that the romance, which contains a number of inconsistencies, is by two authors. A second French romance, also in

fragments, has come down to us in manuscripts of the twelfth
and thirteenth centuries. The author, Thomas, probably lived
in England: his text includes a laudative description of London,
and the language of the manuscripts is tinged with Anglo-
Norman, the variety of Old French peculiar to post-Conquest
England. The romance may have been written for the court of
Henry II, at some time between 1155 and 1170. The fragments
(including one recently discovered in Carlisle) recount the early
stages of the love-affair up to the deception on Mark's
wedding-night, and episodes from the latter part of the story:
the leavetaking in the orchard, Tristran's marriage, his returns
to Cornwall, the death of the lovers. The missing sections of
Thomas' narrative – some three quarters of the whole – can be
reconstructed from thirteenth-century adaptations of it: the
Old Norse *Saga af Tristram ok Isönd*, originally translated at
the Norwegian court of Haakon the Old, the Middle English *Sir
Tristrem* and the most imposing cousin by far in this family of
romances, Gottfried's *Tristan*. 'Thomas von Britanje' is named
by Gottfried in the prologue to his romance as the one
storyteller in the entire tradition who in his judgment told the
story in the right way and on whom therefore he has modelled
his own version (149–62). Gottfried was not the first to
introduce the story to his countrymen, however. An earlier
romance in German, thought to be based on a now lost French
source, is preserved fragmentarily on parchment of the late
twelfth and thirteenth centuries, and entire in paper manuscripts
of the fifteenth. Its author, Eilhart von Oberg, may have been
active around 1190 at the Brunswick court of Henry the Lion,
duke of Saxony; according to an alternative hypothesis he
composed the romance around 1170 in the Lower Rhineland.

Although the earliest romances of Tristan are in French and
German, the story is of Celtic provenance; along with other
Celtic oral traditions, such as tales of King Arthur, it found its
way into French written literature in the twelfth century, and
from there into German. The initial contact between Celtic and
French most likely occurred in Britain and the Breton marches.
There are no surviving Tristan stories in Celtic that predate the
earliest French and German romances; the latter do, however,

contain a number of pointers to their origin. The names of the lovers reflect the Cornish forms *Drystan* and *Eselt* (or Welsh *Essyllt*), and King Mark may owe his name to the Celtic word for 'horse', *march*. (Beroul narrates a bizarre episode in which a dwarf reveals to Mark's nobles that the king has horse's ears.) Thomas mentions a certain 'Breri' as an authoritative source of his information (Douce, 848); possibly this man is the Welsh poet Bleddri ap Cadivor, who may be identical with the famous storyteller mentioned in French and Latin sources by the name Bleheris or Bledhericus. Besides the evidence of names, there is also an indication of Celtic origins in the narrative structure. Old Irish literature has narrative genres known as *immrama*, *tochmarca* and *aitheda*, which treat respectively of sea-voyages, wooings and elopements; these story-types underlie the episodes of Tristan's voyages to Ireland, his winning of Isolde's hand and his flight with her into the forest to escape Mark's wrath (this is how the episode of the cave appears in Beroul and Eilhart). None, however, of the extant Irish stories of these types is a direct source of a Tristan narrative; rather they should be considered as structural analogues which perhaps tell us something about the kind of oral tradition that fed the written romances.

The love potion and the beginnings of love

The lyrics of Chrétien and Veldeke pare down the story of Tristan and Isolde to a single property: the potion that compelled them to love. For modern scholars too this one motif has assumed great importance as a touchstone for identifying different tendencies in the earliest French and German romances. In Beroul and Eilhart the potion's effect wears off after a fixed number of years, three in Beroul, four in Eilhart (who further specifies that during this time the lovers will become ill if they do not see each other every day, and die if they are separated for a whole week; after four years they are freed from these conditions, but remain in love until death) (Beroul, ed. Ewert, 2133–40; Eilhart, ed. Lichtenstein, 2279–99). In the versions of

Thomas and his dependants the potion remains uniformly effective for the lovers' entire lives. Gottfried writes that Isolde's mother 'prepared in a phial a love-potion, so subtly devised and contrived, and endowed with such power, that if any two people drank of it they were bound to love each other alone above all things, whether they wished it or not. To them was given one death, one life, one sorrow and one joy' (11432–44). Simplifying the potion's provisions in this way has the effect of making them more absolute; it is strange, therefore, that so many critics should have maintained that the importance of the potion in Thomas and Gottfried is diminished by comparison with the role it plays in Beroul and Eilhart. The argument is that the versions of the latter two represent an archaic treatment of the story in which the potion is the mechanical cause of love and, at the same time, an exculpatory device: the blame of adultery cannot attach to the lovers, for they had no choice but to love. Thomas and Gottfried are cast as modernizers of the story in whose eyes the potion is an embarrassing and barbaric relic: the idea that love could be caused by drinking a philtre is an affront to the sensibility of the courtly, for whom individual desire and choice are cherished principles (recall again the lyrics). But because the tradition required a potion, the modernizers could not eliminate it altogether. Their solution was, so the argument concludes, to retain it, but stripped of its material efficacy; in their hands the potion became a symbol of a love that has human, psychologically plausible causes which predate the potion's drinking.

This solution to what is imagined to be the modernizing poet's problem, what to do with an unwanted legacy, is hardly free from problems itself. In the case of Thomas, the fragments contain some evidence to suggest that love began before the potion (Tristran alludes to the 'fine and noble love' between him and Ysolt when she cured him of his wound, presumably during his first visit to Ireland), but also evidence implying that the potion causes love (Tristran remarks that he was overcome by love on board ship with Ysolt, and later that he and Ysolt were overtaken by the potion) (Douce, 1219–22; Carlisle, ed. Short, 70). It is no easier to determine whether the potion has any symbolic dimension. Tristran reflects, 'Our death was in the potion, from which we shall never have relief. It was given to us at an evil hour, we drank our death with it' (Douce, 1223–6). The potion is connected with death, but whether as cause or symbol is impossible to tell.

The beginnings of love in Gottfried have been traced back beyond the potion scene to Tristan's earliest encounters with Isolde in Ireland. But all of the evidence cited by interpreters who have scoured these episodes for signs of mutual attraction is susceptible of another interpretation. Examples are the new-found gusto with which the mortally wounded Tristan plays his harp when he sets eyes on Isolde for the first time, and her inability to kill him when she discovers his true identity as the slayer of her uncle Morold. In each case, the text supports an explanation in which love has no part. Tristan puts his heart into his playing because he knows he must ingratiate himself with his audience if he is to be cured (7820–32); the allegorized quality of womanliness which restrains Isolde's rage is not, the context makes clear, tender feelings, but the sense of female decorum (10156–73, 10237–81). Yet even if there is no romantic attachment, conscious or subconscious, between Tristan and Isolde in Ireland, it would be absurd to deny the existence of any relationship at all between them, and equally absurd to deny that the relationship is fraught with the potentialities of a future love. Whoever reads the Ireland episodes already knows from tradition and from Gottfried's prologue that Tristan and Isolde will be lovers, and consequently is alert to hints and forebodings from the narrator. These are present from the outset; when Isolde comes to hear the playing of Tristan, newly arrived in Ireland, she is introduced into the sick-room as 'the true seal of love, with which Tristan's heart was later to be sealed and closed to everyone, except her alone' (7812–16).

Gottfried's language makes it clear that drinking the potion brings about a sea change, putting the protagonists' lives out of joint and transforming them from woman and man into lovers. He explains, 'Now that the maid and the man, Isolde and Tristan, had both drunk the potion, instantly Love, who stirs all and ambushes every heart, was there and stole into the hearts of the two of them' (11707–12). Then Love plants her victory banner in the lovers' hearts and routs the opposing forces of Honour, Loyalty, and Shame. Gottfried concludes this psychomachia, or allegorical war of emotions, with the words, 'The ships put to sea again and sailed joyfully on their way, except that Love had brought two hearts that were on board from their course' (11875–9). The potion, prime mover of this exorbitation, is love's material cause: Gottfried's description, quoted earlier, of its careful preparation leaves no doubt that it is a love-inducing drink. But there is more to it than that. At the ill-starred moment when one of the ladies-in-waiting offers the phial to Tristan in the mistaken belief that it contains wine, the narrator comments: 'No, it was not wine, though it might have resembled it; it was enduring suffering and infinite heartache, of which the pair of them died' (11672–6). The real, winelike liquid cannot literally be suffering and heartache until death; it may cause them (they are the negative half of the 'one death, one life, one sorrow and one joy' said to be the consequences of drinking it), and therefore can be what it causes only in a figurative sense, as a metonym in which the effect is signified by the cause. The strict alternative 'cause or symbol' does not exist for Gottfried, whose potion is both cause *and* symbol of its effects.

Gottfried's likening of the potion to wine prompts comparison with the eucharist. Bread and wine, the physical and visible sacrament, were increasingly interpreted by twelfth-century theologians as symbols of an invisible reality. This symbolic reality was said to consist in the spiritual and salvific union effected by the sacrament between God and the believer or (according to another interpretation) Christ and the church. Opinions differed over whether this union was attainable without receiving the physical sacrament; some theologians held that prayer and meditation could be substitutes for the eucharist, others argued that physical reception was indispensable because it was commanded by the church and brought Christians together in visible unity. This second tendency, which was dominant in the late twelfth and early thirteenth centuries, provides a contemporary analogy for understanding Gottfried's conception of the potion. It is a symbol of a union that nevertheless will not come about unless the two people are physically brought together to partake of the 'wine' in its material guise.

Far from diminishing the potion's importance, Gottfried has increased it by introducing a symbolic dimension. If the allusion to communion wine really is intended, then the love it causes acquires the symbolism of a sacramental union. It is interesting to note the contrast in this respect with Isolde's relationship to her husband Mark. Their marriage really is a sacrament, but Gottfried passes over the ceremony in haste, and does not mention the officiation of a priest, unlike the wedding of Riwalin and Blanscheflur (12544–75; 1630–40). Moreover the wine that Mark and Isolde drink together on their wedding-night is not, Gottfried takes pains to emphasize, the potion, but plain wine (12648–56). It is as though Gottfried has divested the legitimate marriage of its symbolic and sacramental aura, and transferred it to the adulterers Tristan and Isolde.

Love, adultery and marriage

The love of Tristan and Isolde has an indubitable social and moral meaning. It is adultery, a crime which threatens the king's honour, and a sin second only to heresy in gravity. Here above all, perhaps, lies the reason why the story kept being renewed in different versions; it is as though medieval authors and their public were fascinated by the scandalous and intractable theme, and compelled to seek new ways of coming to terms with it.

Tristan and Isolde became a subject for literature in the wake of two developments that had a profound effect on attitudes to sex in western Europe: the revival of canon law, and the church's success in establishing its right of jurisdiction over marriage, divorce and adultery. Canon law, the law of the church, underwent renewal and codification from the beginning of the eleventh century, and by the middle of the twelfth was becoming an academic discipline in its own right, independent of civil law on the one hand and theology on the other. A great deal of canon law is taken up with the regulation of sexual behaviour, with definitions and provisions concerning marriage and marital sex, divorce, adultery, concubinage, fornication, rape, prostitution and the so-called sins against nature. The potential relevance of the new legal scholarship to the Tristan story is obvious: it could and did equip authors, especially clerically educated ones, with a terminology for formulating and probing the questions of legality, sin and morality thrown up by their subject-matter. The canon law revival was part of a movement of reform that had been gathering head inside the church during the eleventh century. The reformers' object was to free the church from secular influence so that it could exercise more effective moral leadership over the whole of society. Canon law supported the church's claim to institutional distinctness and independence, and it set out the Christian norms that the reformers wanted to enforce in the area of sexual behaviour. At the time it was by no means universally accepted that ecclesiastical courts should have sole authority to determine, among other things, whether a marriage was valid and under what circumstances divorce and remarriage might be permissible. Noble families (the only ones for which we have reliable evidence) regarded marriage and divorce as entirely their own business, making and dissolving unions as it suited them. Yet by the middle of the twelfth century the aristocracy in western Europe generally submitted to church jurisdiction in these matters. One of the reasons for their acquiescence was that playing by the church's rules guaranteed indisputably legitimate heirs to whom landed estates and kingdoms could be passed on. Tensions nevertheless persisted, for instance in attitudes to adultery. Secular lawcodes had treated it as a private affair; the offended husband (usually it was female adultery that was criminalized) was entitled to kill the adulterers. For the church, adultery was a matter for the public authorities; it was, above all, a sin to be expurgated by penance, but the fact that throughout the eleventh and twelfth centuries canonists continually forbad Christian husbands to kill their unfaithful wives indicates how ingrained among laymen was recourse to self-help remedies.

This conflict of attitudes is reflected in the forest episodes of Beroul and Eilhart. The king sentences the adulterers to death; they take refuge in the forest, where a hermit admonishes them to repent; the potion prevents them, but once its full effect wanes, they visit him again and declare their remorse. It is as though the adulterers have been transplanted to the place where they will face the church's preferred tribunal. Yet the religious perspective is not followed through, for no penance is imposed and no absolution given. Instead the hermit applies his diplomatic skill to writing a letter on the lovers' behalf that will smooth their return to court. In Beroul he prefaces this course of action with a statement startlingly at variance with his earlier sermonizing, declaring that 'in order to remove shame and cover wickedness one must tell the odd white lie' (2353–4).

Like the hermit, Beroul and Eilhart neither condemn nor commend the lovers entirely. They either overlook the problem of guilt, and concentrate instead on deploring the baseness of the lovers' persecutors, or cite the potion in exculpation. Their narrative technique, which emphasizes the story's extraordinariness and singularity (see below, pp. 37–8), in fact renders categorical judgment of the lovers unnecessary. Sealed in its uniqueness, the lovers' example is incapable of being repeated, and consequently requires neither reproof nor recommendation.

Thomas and Gottfried do not insulate the lovers from the public in this way; on the contrary, they claim that their story possesses an especial moral value for other lovers. Thomas offers them instruction and consolation (Sneyd[2], 835–6), and Gottfried goes further by declaring his romance 'inwardly good' for the noble hearts who make up his chosen public (173). Authors who pretend to the goodness of the Tristan story must come to grips with the objective immorality of the love they celebrate. The solution adopted by Thomas and Gottfried is audacious: the adulterous relationship of Tristan and Isolde displays virtues normally associated with Christian marriage. This vindication of illicit love is not, however, accompanied by a concomitant attempt to denigrate legitimate marriage as a loveless alliance made solely for dynastic and political reasons. True, the romances depict some unhappy marriages (Mark and

Isolde, Tristan and Isolde Whitehand), but there are also counter-examples of marriages founded on mutual affection (Riwalin and Blanscheflur, Rual and Floraete). If there is a contrast in Thomas and Gottfried, it is between relationships lacking reciprocity and those that exemplify the virtues of mutual affection and fidelity without end.

The love of Tristan and Isolde shares at least three specific features with the church's model of marriage: it is an indissoluble and spiritual union; the spiritual union is symbolized by a ring; it is based on the mutual consent of the partners. The co-occurrence of these features, and the precise terminological correspondences, make the parallel too strong to ignore.

(1) *Indissolubility and spirituality*. The love of Tristan and Isolde is permanent and indissoluble, like the marriage-bond. Just as canonists insist that the union continues to exist even when spouses are apart, so Thomas and Gottfried portray a love that transcends the togetherness of the flesh. Ysolt says to Tristran as he takes leave of her: 'Now our bodies must be parted, but nothing will part our love' (Cambridge, 49–50); Gottfried's heroine says in the same situation, 'Tristan and Isolde, you and I, we two are both one inseparable thing for ever' (18352–4). By the later twelfth century most canonists considered the spiritual bond, which existed between a couple from the moment they exchanged vows, to be more important than physical consummation in making a marriage. This spiritualizing trend reflected developments in contemporary theology: in the course of the twelfth century marriage was defined with increasing precision as a sacrament, whose symbolic meaning was, in the words of Hugh of St Victor, the 'mutual love of souls' (*PL* 176, 482). Formulae such as *animorum spiritualis coniunctio*, the spiritual union of souls, or *cordium coniunctio*, the union of hearts, are commonplace in canon law definitions of marriage. Gottfried's commentary on the lovers' first physical union after they have declared their mutual affection contains a strong echo of this spiritual language. 'Love the ensnarer/binder ['strickærinne'] caught/bound together ['stricte'] their two hearts with the snare/bond ['stric']

of her sweetness, with such great skill and such wondrous force
that they were unparted for all their years' (12176–82). The
word *stric* has two meanings and evokes two allusions: in the
sense of 'snare' it is one of those hunting metaphors familiar
from classical erotic poetry (Ovid, for example, depicts the lover
stumbling into the toils of love (*Ars amatoria*, ed. Kenney, III,
591)); its other meaning, 'tie' or 'bond', evokes the terms *ligamen*
and *vinculum* regularly applied by canonists to marriage,
defined in a source contemporary with Gottfried as 'the bond
['vinculum'] that ties ['ligat'] two people reciprocally' (*Ecce vicit
leo*, quoted in Brundage, *Law, Sex, and Christian Society*, p. 352).

(2) *The ring*. This indissoluble and spiritual bond is symbolized
by the wedding-ring. Ivo of Chartres (d. 1116) calls the ring a
sign of mutual love ('mutuae dilectionis signum'), and a token
('pignus') by which the hearts of bride and groom may be joined
(*PL* 161, 586). Rolandus, a mid-twelfth-century canonist,
writes that 'by this ring [...] the union of hearts is symbolized'
(*Summa Magistri Rolandi*, ed. F. Thaner, Innsbruck, 1874, p.
152). Both of these writers quote a tradition whose authority
derives from late antiquity; Isidore of Seville (d. 636) explained
that the ring is worn on the fourth finger because from there the
vein reaches right to the heart (*Etymologiae*, ed. W. M. Lindsay,
Oxford, 1911, XIX. 32.2). According to Gratian, the first
systematizer of canon law around 1140, the ring is above all a
ring of fidelity ('anulus fidei') (*Corpus iuris canonici*, I, 1105);
Rolandus explains that just as the ring has neither beginning
nor end, so the mutual fidelity of husband and wife should be
inviolate, without beginning or end (*Summa*, p. 152).

A ring, given by Isolde to Tristan at their parting, features in
all four early Tristan romances. In Beroul (2711–22) and Eilhart
(9298–9) it functions primarily as proof of identity; when Isolde
sees it she can be sure that the message comes from her absent
lover. Thomas and Gottfried invest this ring with the symbolism
of an 'anulus fidei'. Reversing the usual moral and legal
standards, Thomas' hero considers his legitimate marriage as
infidelity, and his adultery as a relationship imposing a duty of
marital fidelity. The terminology is technical and precise.

Tristran acknowledges the validity of his marriage to Ysolt as Blansches Mains: 'I have married her according to due legal form, at the church door, in the presence of witnesses' (Sneyd[1], 425–6). This refers to the practice, common in France and England from around the middle of the twelfth century, of solemnizing marriages *in facie ecclesiae*, in a public ceremony held at the church door, where a priest officiated as the bride and groom exchanged their vows. Yet the consequences of consummating this valid union are regarded by Tristran as a betrayal of the faith he owes the first Ysolt. A phrase obsessively repeated by him in his tortuous debate on whether to sleep with his wife is *mentir ma fei*; it clearly corresponds to Latin *fidem frangere*, which in the jargon of canonists means 'to commit adultery'. One example, from the early twelfth century, must suffice: 'We call it adultery when, either at the prompting of his or her own desire or with the agreement of another's, a person sleeps with another man or woman against the marital covenant, and thus fidelity is broken ['ita frangitur fides']' (*Sententiae Magistri A.*, ed. H. J. F. Reinhardt, Münster, 1974, p. 183). Tristran's fears about breaking his faith are triggered by the sight of the ring he wears on his finger; it is the ring that Ysolt gave him in the orchard (Sneyd[1], 391–6). It really is an 'anulus fidei'.

The words with which Gottfried's Isolde gives the ring to Tristan are also redolent of canonistic formulations: 'Take this ring, and let it be a token of fidelity and love ['ein urkünde [. . .] der triuwen unde der minne']. If ever you should take it into your thoughts to love something except me, let this remind you how my heart now feels' (18307–14). A few lines later come her words about being one thing without separation or end.

(3) *Consent*. By the end of the twelfth century the church conceived of marriage as a relationship created by the agreement of both parties; it upheld the right of the individual to choose his or her own marriage-partner, even if this went against parental wishes, and it attached great importance to the couple's intentions when determining whether a marriage was valid. The principle that was to remain definitive for most canonists until the Reformation was stated by Pope Alexander

III around 1180: a valid marriage was contracted either if the parties exchanged present consent (that is freely and voluntarily promised to marry each other there and then), or if they exchanged future consent (a promise to marry later; effectively a betrothal) and subsequently ratified that consent by sexual intercourse (*Corpus iuris canonici*, II, 666–7). An exchange of consent between both partners is as important for Thomas and Gottfried as it is for popes and canon lawyers.

Thomas' declaration of love is preserved in the Carlisle fragment. Ysolt declares her feelings equivocally: she complains that she is afflicted by 'lamer', meaning simultaneously 'love' (*l'amer*), 'sea' (*la mer*) and 'bitterness' (*l'amer*). The problem for Tristran is to discover her intention, which he does by responding with an avowal that reduces the polysemy of the word to a single meaning on which he and Ysolt can agree: '"Affliction makes my heart *amer*, and it does not find this malady bitter ['amer'], nor does it come from the sea ['la mer'], but I have this suffering from *amer*, and love has taken hold of me at sea. Now I have said enough to a wise person." When Ysolt hears his thoughts, she is gladdened by the turn of events' (66–73). The word-play is taken over by Gottfried. His account of events from drinking the potion to the lovers' consummation of their passion is around three times longer than Thomas'; the result of this amplification is an even heavier emphasis on consent.

Gottfried states that the potion introduces love into the couple's hearts instantly ('sa') (11709). But because this instant is the most important in the whole story, he does not let it rush by in a sudden flash. It is elaborated and embellished by means of mythology, allegory and metaphor. These are standard poetic devices, which Gottfried has already used to narrate how Riwalin and Blanscheflur fall in love. With them too, love is personified as a powerful and imperious deity (she is Blanscheflur's 'dictatrix' (961)); there is a psychomachia (Riwalin is assailed by doubt and consolation (883–911)); metaphors of snares and bird-lime express the lovers' capture (838–74). With Tristan and Isolde, the effect of these devices is to turn the instant of falling in love into a process. Love, the 'hereditary mistress' of Tristan, overcomes her allegorized opponents Honour, Shame and Loyalty only after these have offered stiff resistance (11756–72, 11822–40); similarly the lovers struggle for a long time to free themselves from the toils or the bird-lime before they admit their capture (11752–5, 11784–814). As well as draw out the moment of falling in love, these devices transfer the process from outside to inside. Potion, mythological and allegorical persons, snares and bird-lime all represent external forces which act upon the human subject, afflicting and entrapping him. At the same time, they all symbolize or personify human affects and emotional states, such as suffering and heartache (the potion's symbolic value), love, honour, shame, loyalty; their interaction creates an inner, psychological drama, the turmoil of the subject pulled this way and that by conflicting impulses until one of them takes possession of him completely. The double perspective, both external and internal, is already visible in Gottfried's initial description of the potion's effect. 'Love the reconciler had purged both their minds of hate, and so united them in affection that each was transparent as a mirror to the other' (11721–6). The agent Love does something to Tristan and Isolde, who are passive objects (neither is the subject of a transitive verb); since, however, the purging is one of minds, these lines can also be read as the description of a psychological process in which the subjects Tristan and Isolde turn feelings of hate to love.

The conversion of an instant into a process and the ambivalence of external and internal points of view are not unforeseen side-effects of the devices Gottfried uses to embellish the potion scene. Rather they are a deliberate strategy for converting externally and accidentally caused love into a relationship founded on mutual consent. Once Tristan and Isolde have succumbed, Gottfried narrates their inward realization of love directly, without any metaphorical disguise: by the physical symptoms of love-sickness 'each recognized clearly, as one must by such things, that his or her thoughts for the other lay in the direction of love' (11921–5). There follows the open declaration, and the consummation, so that by the time Brangaene finally reveals to the lovers that all this was caused by the potion, there can no longer be any question of

their viewing it as a misfortune that has befallen them from
without and paralysed their will. Turning round Brangaene's
ominous statement that the potion is the death of him and
Isolde, Tristan declares, 'Whether it be death or life, it has
poisoned me sweetly. I do not know what the other death will be
like; I find this one delightful. If lovely Isolde is always to be my
death in this way, I would gladly strive to die everlastingly'
(12495–502). Whatever else these words may imply (there has
been a long debate over whether they are blasphemous) they
certainly articulate consent. What Gottfried said about the
potion at the time of its preparation, that to whoever drank it
was given ('gegeben') one life, one death, one joy and one
sorrow, is here willingly accepted by Tristan as a sweet
poisoning ('vergeben'). With his words he pledges himself to an
existence that joins the antitheses of life and death, joy and sorrow.

Interiority

Brangaene's fear for the lovers is founded on a reasonable
assessment of the consequences of drinking the potion. Whatever
Tristan and Isolde do, they are in mortal danger. If they hold
their desire in check, they may die of lovesickness – this is why
Brangaene did not stand in the way of their sleeping together
(12134–6); if they do not hold back, they risk paying with their
lives for adultery. Tristan's riposte sweeps considerations like
these aside, in a manner quite out of keeping with his previous
behaviour in comparable circumstances. He has been poisoned
before, by Morold's sword; the festering wound forces him to
choose: either risk his life to be cured by Queen Isolde, or die
anyway. Possible death seems to him a lesser evil than certain
death, and so he decides to travel to Ireland (7294–322). Now,
however, Tristan is not interested in estimating the objective
risk, but in asserting how this second poisoning feels for *him*.
Gottfried remarks on more than one occasion that lovers are
blind to the facts (15166, 17741–5), or see them in another way
(11856–74); this subjective order of reality constitutes their
interiority.

Interiority is one of the great themes in the revival of intellectual life that has come to be known as the 'renaissance of the twelfth century'. Human nature, its essence and potential became central preoccupations for philosophy and theology; at the same time, literature developed a language for representing and exploring the inner life of the individual. These concerns have affected the early Tristan romances to various degrees. All of them divide the courtly world into two groups: the insiders, who are privy to love's secret, and the outsiders, who are not. The lovers and their confidants meet in private chambers and secluded places, and they communicate by secret signs which they alone recognize. The association of love with the 'inside', with privacy and secrecy, can be carried further: if love takes root inside the characters themselves, and if their state of heart and mind is represented as an order of reality in their own right, then love has become a form of interiority.

Beroul and Eilhart adumbrate the existence of this independent inner state when they remark on the lovers' indifference to the harsh conditions of life in the forest. According to Beroul 'one does not feel it because of the other' (1785); Eilhart observes that 'it was child's play to them, for their great love brought them much joy' (4549–51). Beroul goes no further than adumbration; in fact he implies that the lovers' inner self-sufficiency was really a delusion caused by the potion. As soon as its effect wears off, the lovers feel the prick of conscience; in a series of monologues they lament the discrepancy between their fugitive existence (the asperity of which they now perceive) and the settled life they ought to be leading at court. Tristran regrets that he has neglected chivalry, royal service and lordship; he has wronged his uncle and obliged the queen to exchange her chambers hung with silken curtains for a simple bower. Iseut rues her misspent youth; because of the potion, she has forfeited the name of queen, and lives in the forest like a serf, when she ought to be at court, attended by ladies and marrying them off (2160–216). The sense of self articulated in these monologues is defined by social status and obligations to kin; it is the inner discourse of an apostate lord and lady, not the interiority of lovers.

Unlike Beroul, Eilhart does represent this interiority at

length, in a soliloquy delivered by Isalde after she has drunk the potion. It is characterized by questions, sudden reversals of argument and apostrophes to God, Amor, Cupid, Love and the heart. 'What shall I, poor wretched woman do? I fear he does not desire me; how, then, can I love him? Love? Why do I speak the word? How could I hate him, or ever be his enemy?' 'Alas my lady Love, thanks to what folly did I fall from your grace, so that you make me pay so sorely for your wrath?' 'Now I will try to find a way of putting him out of my thoughts. Heart, you shall think of that valiant man no longer, for I intend to put him out of mind. How could I manage to give him up? I fear it is useless to try; better that I love him' (2410–15, 2505–9, 2560–72). Question and reversal are mimetic devices: their linguistic structures mirror the commotions of a troubled soul; apostrophe, on the other hand, creates the impression of an autonomous self by distancing a beleaguered subject from forces that are perceived as external to it. Together these three rhetorical figures articulate the inwardness of a subject, Isalde, coming to grips with her feelings, reflecting on her situation, and settling on a course of action. The overall movement of her speech is from an initial admission of suffering to the final resolution to declare her feelings, now clarified as feelings of love, to Tristrant; as we follow the train of her thought we trace the emergence of her identity as a lover.

Isalde's soliloquy is the only instance of a long inner monologue in Eilhart, and it so closely resembles a love-plaint in Heinrich von Veldeke's *Eneasroman* that Eilhart is under suspicion of having cribbed it, perhaps in order to make his technique appear modern and sophisticated. That he lacked the necessary competence or interest to develop inner monologue beyond this isolated example is suggested by a comparison with Thomas and Gottfried. The fragments of Thomas show a hero given to agonizing over every aspect of his tangled relationships with women: the dilemma of loving two Isoldes, whether to marry one and forget the other, whether to consummate the marriage. These deliberations assume such large proportions that they actually crowd out external events; Tristran's debate with himself on whether to marry goes on for almost 200 lines, whereas the wedding itself is narrated in a mere fifteen. In Gottfried, whose version covers only the beginning of Tristan's involvement with Isolde Whitehand, the interior monologues plus the narrator's commentary on what is going on inside the hero's head occupy some 400 lines; the action that first brought them together, the feudal war in which Tristan comes to the aid of Isolde's father, is reported in just over 260. By contrast Eilhart devotes around 600 lines to the war, with minimal reporting of the characters' thoughts and feelings, and his breathtakingly rapid account of the marriage (from the initial proposition to one year after the wedding in under thirty lines) concentrates on the negotiations between the men, Tristrant and Isalde's father and brother, rather than explore the hero's feelings for the women.

Thomas and Gottfried not only represent the lovers' interiority more extensively, they develop it into a mode of loving in its own right. One lover is capable of making the absent other present in his or her thoughts and feelings. Gottfried relates that the magical dog Petitcriu, presented to Isolde by Tristan, has a bell which banishes cares; Isolde breaks it off so that she may feel the same sorrow as her absent lover (16359–402). Thomas' heroine similarly endures a self-imposed penance which allows her to share Tristran's sufferings; when he departs, she dons a leather corselet next to her skin, vowing not to remove it until she hears news of him (Douce, 737–99). Finally, Tristran is attracted to marriage because, perversely, it seems to him to offer a way of duplicating Ysolt's situation and feelings in his own life. He resolves to marry Ysolt as Blanches Mains in order to put to the test his suspicion that the first Ysolt has forgotten him for her husband: 'I want to marry the girl in order to know the queen's condition, whether marriage and the conjugal act can make me forget her as she, married to her lord, has come to forget our love' (Sneyd[1], 173–8). The marriage is an experiment, designed to determine whether the queen feels as Tristran fears she does. He is proved wrong on his wedding-night, when the sight of the ring she gave him at their parting reminds him of their love; as penance he resolves to share a bed with his wife, but refrain from intercourse with her (Sneyd[1], 385–588). A still more extreme instance of how the lovers maintain their relationship by inner and imaginary means is Ysolt's delirious insistence that she and Tristran must die one and the same death, no matter how impossible physically. Prevented by a sea-storm from reaching her dying lover, she declares, 'Such is the manner of our love that I cannot feel sorrow without you. You cannot die without me, nor can I perish without you. If I must be shipwrecked at sea, then you will have to drown on dry land' (Douce, 1639–44). An identical death is an assurance of togetherness. Ysolt continues with a fantasy of a common fate beyond their separate drownings: if a fish chanced to swallow them, and somebody caught it and recognized their corpses, they might yet share a sepulchre (1653–62).

So deep is this inward community of Gottfried's lovers that they merge into a single person. Once Tristan and Isolde have drunk the potion 'each was transparent as a mirror to the other. The two of them had one heart; her pain was his hurt, his hurt was her pain' (11725–9). Here togetherness is raised to oneness, mutuality to the reflexive symmetry of images in a looking-glass. Note the chiasmus of 'ir *swære* was sin *smerze*, / sin *smerze* was ir *swære*'. The same formal symmetry is used by Gottfried when he announces the lovers' names for the first time, in the lines of the prologue 'a man a woman, a woman a man, Tristan Isolde, Isolde Tristan' ('ein man ein wip, ein wip ein man, / Tristan Isolt, Isolt Tristan') (129–30); it recurs in the arrangement of the initials T I I T and so on in the acrostic. The principle that one reflects or even is the other provides the ground for the lived identity of the lovers. At their parting, Tristan beseeches Isolde, 'Do not let me out of your heart! You will never leave mine, whatever happens to it; Isolde will always be in Tristan's heart' (18275–9). Her words of reassurance develop the metaphor of dwelling in the other's heart: 'Whether you are near or far, there shall be no life nor any living thing in my heart except Tristan, my self and my life ['min lip und min leben']' (18294–7). The word *lip* means first of all 'body', but also 'life', 'person' and, finally, 'self'. Isolde's following words play on all these meanings: 'One thing I will ask of you: no matter to what corner of the earth you travel, take care of yourself, my self ['min lip'], for if I am bereft of you, then I, who am your self ['iuwer lip'], am dead. For your sake, not mine, I will take care and good wardship of myself, your self ['iuwer lip'], for I know well that your self and your life ['iuwer lip und iuwer leben'] depend on me. We are one self, one life ['ein lip, ein leben'] [...] Tristan and Isolde, you and I, we two are both one inseparable thing for ever' (18334–54). It is easier to grasp the sense of these lines than to translate them adequately: each lover lives in the other, is embodied in the other, *is* in fact the other.

Poetics

The romances of Beroul and Eilhart are more concerned to exteriorize love than to portray its inner and subjective dimension. This concern is manifest both on the level of the plot (the contents of the story) and on the level of narration (the way in which the story is presented). The plot often involves a contest between the lovers, who try to keep their secret, and their adversaries, who seek to bring it into the open. The latter group comprises the hostile barons at Mark's court, their accomplice, the necromancer dwarf who sees the truth in the stars, and the king himself. Their obsession with evidence is shared by the narrators. Beroul and Eilhart concentrate on making things palpable to the senses; they pick out visually striking details, for instance the king turning black with anger or burning with rage like a coal (Beroul, 1068; Eilhart, 4036–7), and they present events as though they were rare and remarkable monuments. The narrative is peppered with formulae of the type 'never did you see (or hear) the like', which emphasize the extraordinariness of the story, and imperatives such as *oez*, *escoutez, vornemet, merkit, hôret*, which enjoin the public to give ear to it. The story is, to borrow a term coined by Alois Wolf, a 'narrative spectacle' (*Mythe*, p. 62). A good example of what this involves is provided by Beroul's account of the lovers' escape from the death sentence imposed on them by Mark. Tristran escapes his captors by making a perilous leap from the window of a chapel high on a cliff; he and Governal ambush the lepers to whom Mark has handed over Iseut, saving her from her grisly fate in the nick of time; together they head for the forest. This dramatic episode begins with the narrator's exclamation 'My lords, hear ['oez'] how our Lord is full of pity' (909–10); similar ejaculations occur throughout the rest of the account, which carries the audience along in high suspense.

This exteriorizing technique is especially suited to oral delivery. Orality is more closely tied to the immediate present than literacy; the spoken word is gone as soon as it has been uttered, and listeners are restricted in their ability to integrate information received at different times. Unlike readers, they cannot turn the pages forward and back in order to cross-check a detail, or resume the story after pausing for reflexion. Consequently what counts in oral performance is the heightening of the present moment through vivid narration of memorable events. This is not to say that the romances of Beroul and Eilhart were necessarily *composed* orally or that they had no readers at all. Both authors position themselves in a book-culture by adducing written sources (Beroul, 1267, 1789; Eilhart, 35, 1314, 4731) or referring to their own work as a book (Eilhart, 9447); the transmission of their romances in manuscript form is proof that they were read. Yet their poetics, with its emphasis on the extraordinary and the memorable, is clearly set towards oral *recital*.

From all that we know of the reception of literature in the twelfth and thirteenth centuries, recital must also have been the main mode of delivery for the romances of Thomas and Gottfried. Yet their poetics definitely solicits the reflexive response that readers are best equipped to give. The story is presented less as a narrative spectacle than as material for the public to absorb and ponder. The poetics of exteriorization is replaced by one of interiorization. This poetics assumes an identity between the fictional characters and the public. Whereas Beroul and Eilhart emphasize how extraordinary the story is, how *unlike* anything the public have seen or heard, Thomas and Gottfried insist on how *like* the characters in the romance their addressees are. They are lovers, hearing or reading about other lovers. Thomas dedicates his work 'to all lovers', in the hope that 'it may please [them], and here and there they may find things to instruct them; may it console them against fickleness and wrong, against suffering and affliction, against all love's wiles!' (Sneyd[2], 821, 833–9). Gottfried similarly offers his story for the delectation of his public, who are designated like Tristan and Isolde as 'noble lovers' ('edele senedære') (121–6). By assuming an identity of interest, Thomas and Gottfried encourage their public to internalize the story, and to compare fictional experience with their own.

As an example of this process let us look at Thomas' commentary on the situation of the characters after Tristran has married and found himself unable to sleep with Ysolt as Blanches Mains. Thomas reflects that all of the protagonists are bound by an 'estrange amor', which has brought each of them nothing but suffering and pain (Turin[1], 71–4). He sums up a lengthy digression as follows: Mark is unhappy because although he has what he desires in Ysolt's body, she does not love him; her situation is wretched because she must consent to conjugal relations with a husband she does not love, while fearing that she may no longer be loved by the man who is her sole desire; Tristran, tormented by the thought that the only woman he desires is with another man, neither loves nor can sleep with Ysolt as Blanches Mains, who for her part is miserable because the love and desire she feels for her husband are not reciprocated (152–79). In the middle of this laborious instantiation of the sufferings of each of the principal characters, Thomas makes a confession: 'As to which of the four of them has the greater torment, I do not know what to say' (144–5). Thus the initial assertion (all four suffer in love) has become a question (who suffers most?). Moreover, it is for those readers or listeners who are lovers to judge which of the four players in this quadrille of misery enjoys the least enviable situation: 'I will put the issue before you; let lovers pass judgment [...] Now whoever knows can give his verdict: which one was happiest in love, or which one had most grief of it' (148–82). Events recede progressively into the background, as narrative gives way to narrator's commentary, and commentary yields in its turn to speculative cogitation on the part of qualified members of the public. Comparison with Eilhart is revealing. He presents the non-consummation of Tristrant's marriage to Isalde as an extraordinary thing standing in need of verification: 'I heard it for the truth that she was with that noble warrior for more than a year but never became his wife' (6138–410). In the hands of Thomas the same situation is not offered to the eyes and ears of the audience as a curiosity, but is dissolved into a set of alternative answers to a speculative question, any of which might be correct. Not only the action is dissolved, so too is the difference between character, narrator and public as all become engaged in the same kind of rumination. The marriage came about because Tristran wondered what it was like for Ysolt to be with her husband; now Thomas ponders which of the four spouses is unhappiest and, declaring himself incompetent to judge, passes the baton to lovers. In all cases, the answer is to be found by trying on possible solutions for size. Tristran marries so that he can experience the queen's situation for himself; Thomas' disquisition on the different permutations of having, desiring and loving is a marshalling of the claims of each of the characters to the prize of being most miserable, which the audience are left to award after duly weighing the merits of each claim. Two verbs that recur throughout the account of the marriage are *assaier* and *esprover*. Tristran decides to marry because 'he wants to try out for himself ['assaier [...] endreit sei'] how Ysolt behaves with the king, and for that reason he wants to test ['assaier'] what pleasure he will have with Ysolt [as Blansches Mains]' (Sneyd[1], 209–12). He asks, 'How can I put this to the test ['esprover'] except by taking a wife? [...] But it ill becomes me to do this at all, except that I want to try ['assaier'] the life [the queen] leads' (163–72). Thomas, summing up, declares that Tristran can find no other reason to marry 'than that finally he wants to test ['assaier'] whether it is possible to have pleasure that goes against love and whether, through the pleasure he seeks, it is possible in time to forget Ysolt' (187–90). The decision about who suffers most is deferred to lovers because, says Thomas: 'I do not know how to give a right answer, because I have not experienced ['esprové'] it for myself' (Turin[1], 146–7).

Thomas maintains a distinction between the literary and the real experience of love, and makes the latter the precondition for judging the former. Gottfried, we shall see in the next chapter, abolishes the distinction. For him too, only those readers or listeners who have a particular experience of love are qualified to understand the story; this experience is, however, created by the story.

Chapter 3

The poet and his fiction

The court, says Hartmann von Aue in the prologue to his Arthurian romance *Iwein* (*c.* 1190/1200), is not what it was in Arthur's time. Yet, he adds, 'I should not want to have lived then, and not be alive now, when their story must still delight us; then they had pleasure by performing the deeds' (ed. G. F. Benecke and K. Lachmann, rev. L. Wolff, Berlin, 1968, 54–8). In refusing to swap a world with fine stories but no fine deeds for one that has the deeds but not the stories, Hartmann expresses his preference for living in the present, when there are two distinct orders of reality: one factual and deficient, the other literary and perfect. The rise of romance in the twelfth century fostered the awareness that literature can make and give access to a reality all of its own; the modern term for this kind of writing, for which the authors of medieval romances had no name, is 'fiction'.

The absence of the word does not mean that the concept did not exist; statements like Hartmann's show that medieval authors did conceive of a specifically literary order of reality. Critical debates have therefore been more concerned with two other questions: how far romance fiction was influenced by Latin rhetoric and poetics, and how different it is from modern literary fiction. On the first point, the Latin term *fictio*, which designates everything invented or figurative, must have been familiar to educated writers; yet this traditional term cannot explain every aspect of romance fiction, for instance the use of narrative structure to create patterns of significance. On the second point, medieval fiction differs tellingly from its modern counterpart by embracing both the imaginary and the historical. Hartmann locates his Arthurian world in the past, and Gottfried insists on the historical underpinnings of his story. By describing the lovers as 'long dead' (222), he implies that they once really existed, and on several occasions he mentions a history-book as the source of his background information (450, 5880, 8942, 15915, 18692). Significantly, though, Gottfried does not claim that everything he says about the lovers is also historical truth.

It does not matter very much whether Hartmann or Gottfried actually believed in the historicity of the characters whose stories they tell. The point is that by presenting them *as though* they once lived, the authors associate romance fiction with remembrance of the past. Invention and memory were in fact allied in medieval conceptions of creativity. Mary Carruthers has highlighted this by comparing contemporary portraits of two outstanding intellectuals from the thirteenth and twentieth centuries, Aquinas and Einstein. The comparison reveals that we moderns do not associate creative genius with memory (we tend to place a low value on the 'mere' memorization of knowledge) whereas Aquinas' brilliance was said to consist in letting his richly retentive memory pour out its treasures (*The Book of Memory*, Cambridge, 1990, pp. 1–7). The intimate connexion between inventiveness and memory holds for medieval literature too. What we keep apart represented two sides of the same coin for medieval poets; remembering and reproducing material from the past – the characters and stories of tradition – was not inimical to imagination and originality. The rhetorical term *inventio*, which means literally 'finding' (the writer finds ideas and words stored in his memory) also means 'invention'. The poet who draws on his memory 'invents', in both senses; the reader who is encouraged to join in this literary memory-work is likewise simultaneously enrolled in an exercise of the imagination.

Gottfried's 'invention' is nowhere more potent and brilliant than in his prologue and literary excursus. These passages deserve close examination, because in them Gottfried sets out his literary programme, calling on an impressive array of models, whose sources range from classical literature and mythology to vernacular poetry and Christian liturgy. Gottfried has been described aptly as 'a man who manipulated models with sovereign skill' (Karl Bertau, *Deutsche Literatur*, p. 919; the phrase is from Walter Benjamin); we shall have cause to admire the range of models Gottfried has at his fingertips, as well as marvel at how he subtly works them into a unique poetics.

The prologue

Classical rhetoric defines the prologue as 'the beginning of an oration by means of which the hearer's mind is disposed to listen' (*Rhetorica ad Herennium*, ed. Caplan, I. 4). Rhetoric taught the orator conventional arguments – topoi – for making the audience well-disposed, complaisant and attentive. These topoi included proverbs and maxims, whose uncontroversial content made them particularly useful to an orator trying to establish common ground with his public. The techniques of oratory were also applied to poetry; sententious reflexions on the obligation to share knowledge, on the need to avoid idleness and the virtue of generosity are the stock-in-trade of writers of literary prologues from antiquity onwards. On the face of things, Gottfried's prologue speaks this language of the commonplace; in fact its 244 lines, alive with the susurrations of other discourses, literary and non-literary, are among the densest and most difficult of the entire romance. We must attune our ears to these whisperings, catch the allusions and appreciate how Gottfried bends them to his own ends, if we are to avoid a superficial reading of his prologue as so much conventional platitude.

Gottfried's prologue may be divided into two on formal grounds. The first part, the strophic prologue, consists of eleven quatrains, each with the same rhyme in all four lines. The remainder, lines 45–244, makes up the stichic prologue, so called because, with the exception of inset quatrains at lines 131, 233 and 236, it is composed like the rest of the work in rhyming couplets. This formal bipartition correlates roughly with Gottfried's purpose, which is also twofold: to make the public well disposed in the manner recommended by the rhetoricians, and to set out his distinctive programme for renewing the story.

Gottfried intimates what kind of public he would like in

strophes 2–10, which in the Heidelberg manuscript begin with
the enlarged initials DIETERIKH. Editors emend 'Kunst' (33)
to 'Cunst', yielding the name Dieterich. If this is the name of
Gottfried's patron, these quatrains are the appropriate place to
discuss what qualities his public should ideally possess, for the
patron is the most important of all those to whom the work is
addressed. The Dieterich quatrains are notoriously difficult,
because Gottfried's language is oblique and in places quite
obscure. The translation is therefore unavoidably also an
interpretation.

The worthy recipient of the work should possess two
qualities, goodwill and discrimination. These are rendered all
the more attractive to the public through being contrasted with
their opposites, wickedness and falsification. Goodwill is the
theme of quatrains 2–4:

> (2) Der guote man swaz der in guot
>   und niwan der werlt ze guote tuot,
>   swer daz iht anders wan in guot
>   vernemen wil, der missetuot.   (5–8)

That person does wrong who does not listen with goodwill to whatever
a good man does with good intentions and solely for the good of the
world.

> (3) Ich hœre es velschen harte vil,
>   daz man doch gerne haben wil:
>   da ist des lützelen ze vil,
>   da wil man, des man niene wil.   (9–12)

A great deal of what one in fact wants to have I hear being falsified; the
consequences are an excess of smallness and wanting what one does
not want.

> (4) Ez zimet dem man ze lobene wol,
>   des er iedoch bedürfen sol,
>   und laze ez ime gevallen wol,
>   die wile ez ime gevallen sol.   (13–16)

It is proper for a man to praise what, after all, he does need, and he
should let it please him for as long as it comes his way.

'Der guote man' evokes Quintilian's definition of the orator as a *vir bonus* (*Institutio oratoria*, ed. Butler, II.15.1, 33) and therefore can stand for an author, Gottfried for instance. The allusion and the context, a prologue introducing a work of literature to its public, enable us to read into the extremely general phraseology of quatrain (2) a specific meaning: a work written in good faith and in the best interests of the audience deserves their favour. Consequently, the two reactions to what is done with good intentions, showing goodwill and withholding it, are two responses to literature. The negative reaction is stigmatized as maleficence ('missetuon') and falsification ('velschen'). Persistent falsification, the refusal to recognize what is truly desirable, leads to an excess of smallness, because by this attitude greatness is made to appear trivial or nugatory (this is my attempt to understand the obscure wording of lines 9–11); it also entails falsification of one's real desires, an illogical wanting what one does not want. Notice that a third attitude is not mentioned, namely that one might bestow disfavour on something done in bad faith. This omission suits Gottfried; if he can make his public swallow the premise that his intentions are good (and it would take a brave man to impute the opposite to him), they are left with little choice but to show him favour.

The next quatrain turns to the quality of discrimination:

(5) Tiur unde wert ist mir der man,
    der guot und übel betrahten kan,
    der mich und iegelichen man
    nach sinem werde erkennen kan. (17–20)

I hold that man in high esteem who can distinguish good from bad and recognize me and every man for what he is worth.

Anyone who is prepared to suggest that Gottfried might be bad risks denunciation as a wicked falsifier of the good; it is safer, therefore, to take on trust the author's good intentions, acclaim him, and count oneself among his valued friends. As an exhortation to exercise discrimination these lines cannot be taken seriously; they are an invitation to self-flattery, which Gottfried indulges further in the two following quatrains, where it is stated that those who show favour cause art to thrive:

> (6) Ere unde lop diu schepfent list,
>   da list ze lobe geschaffen ist:
>   swa er mit lobe geblüemet ist,
>   da blüejet aller slahte list.   (21–4)

Honour and praise create art, where art is created worthy of praise; wherever it is garlanded with praise all manner of art flourishes.

> (7) Reht als daz dinc zunruoche gat,
>   daz lobes noch ere niene hat,
>   als liebet daz, daz ere hat
>   und sines lobes niht irre gat.   (25–8)

Just as a thing falls into neglect if it has neither praise nor honour, so a thing gives pleasure when it is honoured and not denied its praise.

These lines expand Cicero's dictum 'Honour nourishes the arts' (*Tusculan Disputations*, ed. J. E. King, London, 1927, I. 2). Gottfried goes further: praise *creates* the arts. Like the falsifiers of quatrain (3), those who withhold praise are malefactors, and the charge against them now is that their attitude brings about the neglect of art. Once again Gottfried comments on reactions to an object assumed to be good; the formula 'where art is created worthy of praise' touches on the possibility that art is produced that is unworthy of praise, but this is not developed. We shall see that in the literary excursus Gottfried is not above disparaging what he considers bad art; at this very early stage in the work, however, when he is still unsure of his public, this is an option he would do well not to promote.

As honour and praise create art, so falsification and malevolence blight it:

> (8) Ir ist so vil, die des nu pflegent,
>   daz si daz guote zübele wegent,
>   daz übel wider ze guote wegent:
>   die pflegent niht, si widerpflegent.   (29–32)

Nowadays there are so many people who cultivate the habit of considering good things bad, and bad things good; theirs is no cultivation, but its opposite.

(9) Cunst unde nahe sehender sin
    swie wol diu schinen under in,
    geherberget nit zuo zin,
    er leschet kunst unde sin.   (33–6)

However well art and connoisseurship get along in harmony, if
malevolence comes to dwell in their midst it will extinguish art and
discernment.

Translation cannot capture fully the play on *pflegen* and
widerpflegen (the latter a nonce-word of Gottfried's). *Pflegen*
means both 'to do habitually' and 'to nurture'; the habit of
falsifiers is a perverse cultivation, a destructive and malevolent
widerpflegen that spells the end of art.

   The tenth quatrain rounds off the Dieterich sequence with a
peroration echoing Christ's words in Matthew 7: 13–14: 'Wide
is the gate, and broad is the way, that leadeth to destruction,
and many there be that go in thereat [...] strait is the gate, and
narrow is the way, which leadeth unto life, and few there be that
find it.'

(10) Hei tugent, wie smal sint dine stege,
     wie kumberlich sint dine wege!
     die dine stege, die dine wege,
     wol ime, der si wege unde stege!   (37–40)

O virtue, how narrow are your paths, how arduous your ways! Blessed
is he who walks your paths and ways!

There is a further scriptural echo, of the first psalm 'Blessed is
the man that walketh not in the counsel of the ungodly, nor
standeth in the way of sinners.' But Gottfried's prologue is no
religious homily, his theme is not the soul's perdition, but the
corruption of value and the destruction of art. If he resorts to
biblical language, then for its connotations of good and evil,
virtue and sin, salvation and damnation; the strong feelings of
sympathy and revulsion these will provoke are orchestrated by
him the more effectively to lead his public down the path of
favour.

   The Dieterich quatrains offer more than a description of an
ideal public; they attempt, by means of persuasive and emotive
language, to *create* such a public. They are a dazzling instance

of what rhetoricians call *captatio benevolentiae*, a strategy calculated to deliver goodwill. The handbooks of rhetoric equip the orator with a whole armoury of techniques whereby he can ingratiate himself with his public. He can present himself as a worthy man to whom a favourable hearing is only due – recall Gottfried's insinuation that he is the good man; he can flatter his audience, as Gottfried panders to the discriminating listener or reader; he can denigrate his opponents, cowing his audience into complaisance lest by objecting they should tar themselves with the same brush as these despicable characters: compare here Gottfried's caricature of the falsifying, maleficent and malevolent critic. Cicero declares that the orator's first duty is 'to adapt speech to persuasion' (*De oratore*, ed. Sutton/Rackham, I.31.38); these quatrains of Gottfried's are quintessential rhetoric, a subtle browbeating of the public which deploys every trick in the book.

In the rest of the prologue the emphasis shifts from inculcating the desired attitude to the good upon its recipient to the good itself. In four models of literary communication, each new one modifying its predecessor, Gottfried sets out the conditions under which the story, assumed to be good, will be renewed by him for the good of his public. It is fitting that this discussion should take place in the portions of the prologue that begin in the Heidelberg manuscript with the initials of his name and those of the lovers: G (line 1), T (41), I (45).

(1) *The story as remembrance*. The prologue commences with a maxim on memory. In most of the manuscripts (whose reading I prefer to Ranke's edition) the opening quatrain reads:

> (1) Gedæhte man ir ze guote niht,
> von den der werlde guot geschiht,
> so wærez allez alse niht,
> swaz guotes in der werlde geschiht. (1–4)

If one did not hold dear the memory of those by whom the world has benefited, then whatever good things happen in the world would be as nothing.

This is an example of the *memoria* topos, the routine and

conventional expression of the idea that remembrance is a necessary, honourable and indeed profitable undertaking. The topos is current among classical and medieval historians, who present their discipline as *memoria rerum gestarum*, the remembrance of deeds which, if they are not forgotten, will continue to benefit the present. For, as Cicero says, 'history is the teacher of life' (*De oratore*, II. 36).

In these lines Gottfried associates memory, oblivion and profitability in the conventional manner of the historians; unlike the historiographical *memoria* topos, the quatrain does not, however, specify what it is that should be remembered, or who should do the remembering on which the continued survival and effectiveness of the good depends. Gottfried may be insinuating that his public should remember him, who is telling the story for their profit and has thereby earned his place in the ranks of those who have benefited the world. That would lead smoothly into the following quatrain, where he implies that he is the well-intentioned good man. Interpreted thus, the quatrain is part of the strategy of wooing the public. Alternatively the object of commemoration might be the lovers or their story, not yet named but which, once revealed, are said to do good (172, 222–5); Gottfried may mean that he as author should not forget them, thus vindicating his project from the outset as a necessary act of preserving the good for posterity, or he may mean that his public should remember the lovers and their story for the good it will do them. There is no need for us to choose any one of the possible interpretations to the exclusion of others; what matters is that among the several meanings that might reasonably be assigned to this indeterminate statement about the importance of memory is the proposition that telling and hearing a story involve remembrance.

(2) *The story as occupation.* Remembrance is made more precise in the passage immediately following the Dieterich quatrains (41–171). Memory is reformulated as an occupation ('unmüezekeit') carried out diligently by the author, who has researched the story of the noble lovers ('edele senedære') Tristan and Isolde in all kinds of book; he presents the fruits of

his reading to a particular public, the noble lovers ('edele senedære') or noble hearts ('edele herzen'), who are in their turn to occupy themselves ('unmüezic wesen') with the story. The vague notion of profit is also made more specific; the love story will bring comfort to the noble hearts who, like Tristan and Isolde, suffer for love.

The idea of the story as occupational therapy for heartsore lovers is taken from Ovid. In the *Remedia amoris*, Ovid's treatise on cures for love, unhappy lovers are advised to shun idleness and lose themselves in occupation; on no account, however, should they occupy themselves with love poetry, for this will only make the pain worse (ed. Kenney, 136–44, 757–8). Gottfried prescribes the very activity Ovid forbids; he can do this because his programme of therapy is directed at a quite different sort of patient with a quite different sort of malady. Ovid's addressees are casualties of love, who seek an end to their suffering; this love is an art which can be both learned (from Ovid's own *Ars amatoria* for instance) and unlearned again (the purpose of the *Remedia*). Gottfried on the other hand writes for confirmed lovers and conceives of love as a permanent condition. Anticipating the objection that a love story is not a fit occupation for lovers, Gottfried counters that noble hearts are so addicted to their passion that even its pain is a source of delight to them; therefore they welcome stories which cause the flame of love to burn more intensely (101–22). The consequence of Gottfried's difference with Ovid is that his occupational therapy can offer only a half-cure ('halbe senfte') (75). The story does not remove suffering, but stimulates it; yet this suffering is immediately halved because for the noble hearts it is also pleasure.

A great deal has been written about the 'edele herzen': whether the term is modelled on the *edeliu sêle* of mysticism, the noble soul of the adept who achieves union with God, or whether instead it reflects a purely secular concept, the courtly ideal of the *gentil cuer* or the *nobilitas cordis* praised in ancient ethics. Whatever its antecedents and analogues may have been, Gottfried uses the name to designate a public whose particular experience of love sets them apart from the common run of men. The latter 'cannot bear any suffering and want only to glide along in joy' (52–3); these are people who would reach for one of Ovid's cures as soon as love turned sour. The noble hearts, by contrast, belong to another world, one that 'bears together in one heart its sweet bitterness, its dear sorrow, its heart's desire, its love's anguish, its dear life, its sorrowful death, its dear death, its sorrowful life' (59–63). These are the candidates for Gottfried's half-cure; their bittersweet experience will be simultaneously inflamed and assuaged by a story in which the lovers experience the same mixture of joy and sorrow. Blanscheflur feels 'the sweet heartache that torments many a noble heart' (1073–5); Riwalin discovers 'that the heart's desire could also be such touching pain' (919–20); Tristan and Isolde would not be celebrated lovers 'if in one heart they had not borne sorrow and languorous lament for the sake of love and heartfelt bliss' (212–14).

The characteristic experience of the noble hearts, which they share with lovers in the story, is expressed by the rhetorical figure of oxymoron. This is a favourite stylistic device of Gottfried's; he uses it to express all manner of paradoxes, but above all to find words for the paradoxical experience and nature of love, that 'sweet sorrow which works such miracles as turning honey to gall, sweet to sour, dewdrops to fire, balm to pain' (11882–7). The rhetoric can be interpreted either as a reflexion of lived experience (oxymoron imitates the bittersweet reality of love) or as productive of experience (one could not recognize what one feels as bittersweet if oxymoron did not first exist). Just as the rhetoric of the Dieterich quatrains creates the ideal recipient for Gottfried's work, so figures such as oxymoron may create the lover's identity. Rather than think of the noble hearts as an elite who bring their real experience of love to the story, as Thomas encourages his audience to do (above, pp. 39–41), we might imagine them as a group who take their name and their defining experience from the story. The identity of experience that joins them to the lovers in the story would be created by occupying themselves with the work, which induces a pleasurable pain. It is interesting that wherever in the prologue Gottfried refers to reading, as distinct from hearing, the story, in the same breath he also mentions noble hearts. 'Of my own free will I present my reading of this love story to all noble hearts for their occupation; it is very good reading for them' (167–72); the lovers' story 'is bread for all noble hearts [...] we read their life, we read their death' (233–5). It may begoing too far to see the noble hearts exclusively as readers, but we should consider the possibility that one becomes a noble heart in virtue of the ability and inclination to occupy oneself with Gottfried's poetic language.

(3) *The story as school of virtue*. The story is recommended to the noble hearts as 'very good reading' which can 'impart virtues to life' (172–5). The previous two models had been concerned with the relationship between the past (Tristan and Isolde) and the present (the condition of the noble hearts); this one, which suggests that the story can help its public to lead better lives, looks to the future. The sum of all three models is this: remembrance preserves past good so that it may create future good in the lives of those who occupy themselves with it.

This is not a simple didactic model of the kind that considers literature's work as done when its examples are imitated in life (Conrad of Hirsau, for instance, the author of a twelfth-century manual of literature, defines the 'final profit' of reading as 'the improvement of the reader's character, for if you do not imitate the good you read, the exercise of reading is in vain' (*Dialogus super auctores*, ed. R. B. C. Huygens, Leiden, 1970, p. 83)). Having praised the story and love itself as the font of all virtue (174–90), Gottfried laments his contemporaries' unwillingness to give their all for love. 'Since love produces so many virtuous lives, since so much virtue comes of it, alas! that everyone alive does not strive after heartfelt love ['owe daz allez, daz der lebet,/ nach herzeliebe niene strebet'], that I can find nobody ['daz ich so lützel vinde der'] willing to bear pure heartfelt desire in his heart for the sake of a loved one' (191–7). The scope of these lines is difficult to determine; 'allez, daz der lebet [...] niene strebet' could be interpreted as either 'every single person alive does not strive' or 'not everyone strives'; 'so lützel [...] der' might mean 'so few individuals' or, because *lützel* can also mean 'none', 'nobody at all'. The story's chances of having an improving effect on its public are slim, possibly non-existent. Even if we take the optimistic interpretation, which concedes that a very few people (the noble hearts?) remain receptive to a programme of moral invigoration, it is interesting that the reward Gottfried promises is essentially literary. People nowadays, he complains, are not prepared to accept that love entails suffering; yet 'with these two things one must achieve honour and praise, or without them perish. If those of whom this love story tells had not borne in one heart sorrow and languorous lament for the sake of love and heartfelt bliss, their name and their story would not be a blessing and delight for many a noble heart' (208–17). The prize won by Tristan and Isolde for loving virtuously is to qualify for entry into literature. Didactic writing achieves its goal when good literature is embodied in life, but Gottfried puts the emphasis on how a good life is turned into literature. It is as though he were more interested in the medium than in the realization of its message. What began as the citation of a standard didactic model of reading is developed by the next model into a vision of how a virtuous life, which will always end in death, can assume new life inside the experience of literature.

(4) *The story as sacrament*. The contrast between Gottfried's contemporaries and the exemplary behaviour of Tristan and Isolde opens up a gap between present and past. That gap is what makes the story so valuable; it is a reminder of what very few, or maybe no people possess: 'Even nowadays it is pleasing for us to hear about the lovers' inmost loyalty, sweet and ever new, their joy, their sorrow, their bliss, their distress' (218–21). No longer will the public be improved by the story, they will simply be pleased by it. The virtues that the story imparts to life have become purely aesthetic; the identity of noble hearts and the noble lovers Tristan and Isolde is to be renewed not in practice, but for the duration of the story, which is offered as a sacrament.

Whenever the story of Tristan and Isolde, their joy and their sorrow, is read aloud, it is as sweet bread for all noble hearts (230–3). Hearing the story has become a rite akin to the sacrament of the eucharist. The liturgical inspiration for Gottfried's final model of literary communication explains, I think, why at this point he describes the reception of his work as 'hœre[n] lesen' (230); the tale is read out, as the mass is read from a missal. The allusion to the eucharist is plain; one need only recall the words of Christ 'I am the bread of life [. . .] If any man eat of this bread, he shall live for ever' (John 6: 48–51). The twelfth century was the period when theologians were giving definitive shape to the doctrine of the eucharist, a shape that, once it was set by the Albert the Great, Aquinas and Bonaventure in the thirteenth century, would hold until the Reformation. Theological discussions emphasize repeatedly the sweetness and life-giving power of the host. Lothar dei Conti, the future pope Innocent III, calls the eucharist a 'most sweet syrup' (*PL* 217, 884); James of Vitry (*c.* 1160/70–1240) writes that 'by tasting Christ we all recover life' (*Historia occidentalis*, ed. J. F. Hinnebusch, Fribourg, 1972, p. 208), and Bonaventure describes the communicant as 'the taster of the sweetness of the sacrament and of love' (*Sermones dominicales*, ed. J. G. Bougerol, Grottaferrata, 1977, p. 265).

It is worth examining the closing lines of the prologue closely, because they show Gottfried's rhetoric at its most productive and vertiginous. The words *leben* and *tôt*, life and death, are repeated over and over in varying configurations to incantatory, almost mantric effect, and in being so repeated and rubbed against each other they cease to be opposites. 'Although they are long dead, yet their sweet name lives' (222–3). Here 'dead' stands for physical extinction, whereas 'living' refers not to biological existence, but the afterlife conferred by the continuing celebration of the dead lovers in literature. This distinction, the one term used literally, the other figuratively, is elided in the next two lines. 'May their death live long and for ever, for the good of the world' (224–5). This could mean: may the circumstances of the lovers' physical death be kept alive in the retelling. But if one understands 'death' not as literal dying, but as a metaphor for the literary afterlife (the time when Tristan and Isolde are physically dead is the period when they live in literature), the distinction between life and death begins to be eroded: may their death, which is their life in literary commemoration, live. From here it is a short step to maintaining that death can give life. 'Their death must ever be life and renewal for us who are alive' (228–9). As bread for all noble hearts, the death of Tristan and Isolde lives (233–4). The two words, life and death, have become so entangled that Gottfried can say 'We read their life, we read their death' (235), suggesting by the parallelism of the clauses that reading the lovers' life is the same thing as reading their death. In the prologue's penultimate quatrain death is life, life is death, each term standing for the other. 'Their life, their death are our bread. Thus their life lives, thus their death lives. Thus they live though they are dead, and their death is bread for the living' (237–40).

The eucharistic analogy in which Gottfried's prologue culminates has long been recognized for what it is; it has been recognized too that it is related to the *memoria* topos with which the prologue begins. The eucharist is a rite of commemoration; when instituting it, Christ enjoined the disciples to 'Do this in remembrance of me' (Luke 22: 19). These words are the point of departure for twelfth-century theological discussions of the eucharist as commemoration. Lothar dei Conti asserts that 'the sacrament of the altar is the commemoration of Christ's death [...] In this sacrament the memory of Christ's death is daily renewed for us' (*PL* 217, 883). Lothar's treatise, written around 1195, was not the first to describe the eucharist as commemoration and renewal. Early in the twelfth century Rupert of Deutz (1079–1135) had written, in terms redolent of the historians' topoi of memory and oblivion, that 'if that which thanks to the sacrament is now warm everywhere grows cold, namely Christ's memory, universal love will grow cold, faith become dumb, hope falter [...] Therefore if such exalted memory remains warm, the love of Christ is warm too, the building of faith stands firm upon its foundation, hope comes back to life in the daily remission of our sins' (*PL* 170, 42–3). It is easy to multiply these examples; they reveal that it cannot be by chance that Gottfried should end a prologue that begins with the word 'Gedæhte', from *gedenken*, 'to remember', with an allusion to the eucharist.

The eucharist commemorates a past event, Christ's passion,

and it exemplifies the creative power of words. It is the words of consecration, spoken by the priest, that cause bread and wine to become body and blood. Peter Comestor (d. *c.* 1179) puts it starkly: 'When these words are uttered, This is my body, this is my blood, transubstantiation occurs by the power of these words' (*PL* 198, 1618). It is precisely because the eucharist unites memory with an affirmation of the transformative potential of language that Gottfried adopts it as the final model for his poetic renewal of the story of the long dead lovers Tristan and Isolde.

In the eucharist Christ's body, made present in the host, is eaten by the communicant. But, writes James of Vitry, 'this food is not for the body, but the soul, not for the flesh, but the heart' (*Historia occidentalis*, p. 214). As spiritual food, the eucharist is similar to reading-matter, which is regularly described as food for the mind; Lothar indeed describes the sacrament as a substitute for reading. He writes that scripture, the Word, is 'nourishment for the very few and for the mind alone'; Christ, on the other hand, 'who assumed body and soul in order to cure both body and soul, by the provident art of his charity compounded ointments with which he might destroy the sick man's drowsiness of spirit in the daily renewed commemoration of his salvation, and with which, by means of this most sweet syrup confected in the sacrament of bread and wine, to accustom the toothless people to sip, people that is who lacked teeth to chew the solid food, as it were, of the ancient word and eternal beginning' (*PL* 217, 884). Whereas Lothar distinguishes between the word and the sacrament, Gottfried joins them, for his words are the sacrament; whereas Lothar insists that the eucharist is available even to the ignorant, Gottfried reserves the sweet bread of his story for those who are particularly attuned to the qualities of his writing. In reading the life and death of Tristan and Isolde, bodily present in the bread of the story, noble hearts are called to life and kept alive. The literary word commemorates, calls the dead back to life, renews and sustains. It is, I think, hard to imagine a more breathtaking appropriation of religious language in order to promote the status and the power of literary fiction.

The literary excursus

In the prologue Gottfried displays confidence in the power of his fiction to call to life the long-dead lovers, Tristan and Isolde, for the sake of an audience of noble hearts whose sense of identity may equally be the creation of the author's sovereign command of words. His own importance as the maker of such potent fiction he keeps hidden behind declarations of good intentions and ministering to his public's needs. That is a wise tactic: boasting will not endear him to an audience of whose goodwill he is not yet assured. But later on in the work Gottfried reveals himself as anything but modest about his talent. The passage in question is the so-called literary excursus, a gallery of poets in which Gottfried holds up to scrutiny the eloquence of some of his predecessors and contemporaries, dispensing praise and blame according to how far it matches his own ideal of literary style. This long digression is embedded into the account of Tristan's investiture as knight. At first sight the train of thought appears to roam from one thing to the next without much connexion between the individual parts: narration of the accolade, modesty topos, poets' gallery, prayer to the Muses, description of Vulcan and Cassandra. On closer inspection however it becomes clear that Gottfried never slackens his control over the entire passage, which is bound together by a continuity of theme and imagery. Two of its constituent elements, the modesty topos and prayer for inspiration, are stock devices of literary prologues, and Gottfried's excursus is in effect a continuation of his prologue. Here he gives notice that he possesses the necessary skill for renewing the story along the ambitious lines laid down in the prologue; here, in a remarkable display of self-possession, he emerges from behind the self-effacing disguise he had donned earlier.

(1) *Allegory of the four splendours* (4555–88). Gottfried narrates how new clothes for the thirty companions who are to be dubbed knights with Tristan are made by four 'splendours'. The qualities that go to make perfect knightly apparel (and the

perfect knight and courtier) are personified and portrayed as a team who collaborate in the creation of knightly apparel: 'Elevation of Spirits desired, Wealth provided, Sagacity wove and cut, Courtliness sewed clothes for all of them' (4575–8). With this allegory Gottfried lays the ground for the discussion of literary style that will follow: weaving, dyeing and cutting cloth are age-old metaphors for poetic composition.

(2) *Narrator's question* (4589–96). 'Now that the companions have been made ready in seemly splendour, how shall I set about speaking so as to prepare their noble captain Tristan for his accolade in such a way that people will hear what I say with pleasure and it will suit the story well?'

We are familiar from Thomas' romance with the device of interrupting the narrative with a question. Whereas the question posed by the narrator there afforded him and his audience an opportunity to speculate about what it is like to be in love (above, pp. 39–40), the problem put forward by Gottfried for consideration here is of an entirely literary nature: how to find agreeable words that will sit well on his story, as the splendid clothes befit their wearers and the occasion of their wearing. Gottfried alludes to two of the cardinal requirements of stylistic ornament laid down by rhetoric and poetics: *delectatio* and *decorum*. Style is effective when it is agreeable and when it is apt, suited to its subject-matter, that is, as well as to the audience and the circumstances. By asking aloud how he can meet these requirements, Gottfried has set himself the task of proving to his public the effectiveness of his eloquence.

(3) *Narrator's embarrassment* (4597–620). Gottfried does not boast openly of his skill; on the contrary, he protests his incapacity: 'On this topic I do not know what I may say that would be pleasant and agreeable for you and fitting adornment for this story' (4597–9). He fears that his intellect and his tongue, his faculties of invention and eloquence, cannot compete with the many other writers who have excelled him in the description of knightly splendour. 'If I had at my disposal twelve intellects instead of my one, and if it were possible for me

to have twelve tongues in my one mouth, each of which could speak as I can, still I should be unable to come up with a good description of splendour such that nobody had done it better' (4604–15). Plurality of tongues is a metaphor for powerful eloquence in classical literature. Virgil's Sibyl, for instance, employs it in order to emphasize the sheer impossibility of giving Aeneas an exhaustive account of the torments suffered by sinners in Tartarus: 'If I had a hundred tongues, a hundred mouths, and a voice of iron, I could not encompass every form of crime, nor mention every punishment's name' (*Aeneid*, ed. R. A. B. Mynors, Oxford, 1969, VI, 625–7). The high literary pedigree of Gottfried's modesty topos gives the lie to his embarrassment; his denial of his skill is executed with considerable resourcefulness. He continues: 'Truly the adornments of chivalry have been described in so many ways and are such a well-worn topic of eloquence that I am incapable of discoursing upon it so as to give any heart joy' (4616–20). These words may contain a note of disdain for the trite theme of chivalric pomp, so that Gottfried is setting himself above the subject which he claims overwhelms him; certainly there is an irony to the whole modesty topos, for in the rest of the passage Gottfried will display powers of invention that leave him quite on top of the subject, and he will give evidence of an eloquence that outdoes the predecessors whose example is supposed to have undermined his faith in himself.

(4) In the *gallery of poets* (4621–820) Gottfried names some of those confreres whose eloquence he professes to admire. Unlike him, they are in full possession of their faculties, and their diction is agreeable and apt. Heinrich von Veldeke is lauded for speaking with consummate artistry, the eloquence of Bligger von Steinach is delightful, his genius enchanted by fairies, his tongue a harp on which words and meanings are played in harmony. As to Hartmann von Aue, the laureate, Gottfried marvels 'how he dyes and adorns his stories right through, inside and out, with words and meanings! [...] How limpid, how pure his delicate crystal words are; may they ever be so! They approach their listener in seemly fashion, draw close to

him and give pleasure to right minds' (4622–33). Perspicuity, the hallmark of an apt style, is achieved by the congruent adornment of words and meanings; in the words of Geoffrey of Vinsauf, a teacher of poetics contemporary with Gottfried, 'a speech must always be coloured within and without [...] In what you will have said be like Argus and look round with keen eyes for words to suit your proposed theme' (*Poetria nova*, in *Les arts poétiques du XIIe et du XIIIe siècle*, ed. E. Faral, Paris, 1924, p. 220). Delight and decorum continue to be the keynotes in Gottfried's paean to the 'nightingales', his term for the minnesingers. They do the heart good with their singing and are all adept at their office (4756–61), just as the four splendours were said to be potent in theirs (4566). Reinmar von Hagenau is credited with the tongue of Orpheus; the song of Walther von der Vogelweide hails from 'Zytheron', seat of the goddess of love. Mount Cithaeron is one of the homes of the Muses, but Gottfried has confused it with Cythera in Crete, a centre of the cult of Aphrodite. The confusion may be deliberate conflation, in order to suggest that Walther's singing is doubly inspired, by the Muses, to whom Gottfried will shortly consider directing a prayer, and by Love, the tutelary deity of the grotto to which Gottfried's hero and heroine will later retire.

The change of theme in the gallery, from knightly adornment to stylistic ornament, is made smooth by the continuity of cloth-working imagery. Gottfried's generic term for the narrative poets is *verwære*, 'dyers'. Hartmann, we saw, colours his stories within and without; Bligger's words are woven out of gold and silk thread and artfully fringed, his genius is such that it must have been spun by fairies, and the product of his marvellous eloquence is a work entitled 'The Tapestry' (this allusion is our only evidence for a work of Bligger's by this name) (4694–713). Heinrich is complimented for 'cutting his meaning so beautifully' (4729). Into his gallery Gottfried also introduces some new imagery for discussing the ornaments of style. Heinrich is commemorated above all for grafting the first twig of eloquence on the now flourishing tree of German literature. From that tree Gottfried and his contemporaries 'pluck the perfection of flowers and twigs in the way of words and melodies' (4748–50).

The rhetorical figures with which an author decked out his language were often referred to as *flores*; anthologies of choice specimens of style culled from various poets were known as *florilegia*. In this context, 'picking flowers and twigs' is a metaphor for adorning one's style. The floral imagery comes into its own in the discussion of the anonymous poet singled out by Gottfried for vituperation.

The hare's companion (probably Wolfram von Eschenbach, see above, p. 8) and others like him 'afford us shade with a tree-trunk, not with the green foliage of Maytime, not with twigs and not with branches. Scarcely ever does their shade soothe the eyes of anyone who sojourns there. To tell the truth, their words provide nothing by way of contentment or pleasure for the heart; the hue of their eloquence would never win a noble heart's smile' (4673–82). The image of the trunk derives, directly or indirectly, from Lucan, who likens Pompey to an aged and barren oak which 'casts shade not with leaves, but with its trunk' (*Bellum civile*, ed. A. E. Housman, Oxford, 1926, I, 140). Lucan's simile is also used by Peter Abelard to convey the overblown reputation and intellectual sterility of his opponent Anselm of Laon (*Historia calamitatum*, ed. J. Monfrin, Paris, 1967, p. 68). Sterility of invention and barrenness of meaning are likewise evoked by Gottfried's image of the leafless trunk of eloquence with its inhospitable shade. The exponents of such eloquence are disparaged as 'story-hunters' (4666) who 'must have their tales accompanied by interpreters. We cannot understand them by what we hear or read, nor do we have the leisure to hunt out the glosses ourselves in black books' (4684–90). Quintilian warns against obsolete words which will make one's style obscure 'as though an author had scoured the records of the priests, the oldest treaties and the works of long-forgotten writers with the purpose of collecting words that nobody understands' (*Institutio oratoria*, VIII.2.12). Obscurity can also result from inept metaphors or an injudicious use of hyperbaton, the transposition of words out of their normal order. These abuses are, I think, at the base of Gottfried's accusation that the hare's companion 'jumps high and hunts far and wide on the word-heath with his dice-words ['bickelworten']'

(4641–2). Cicero warns that 'far-fetched metaphors are to be avoided' (*De oratore*, III.41.163), and the *Rhetorica ad Herennium* counsels restraint in the use of metaphor, lest the orator should appear 'to have rushed into an unlike thing' (IV.24.45). 'Bickelwort' is a hapax legomenon. It might be derived from *bickel*, 'pick', meaning that inept words are jagged and sharp; a derivation from *bickel*, 'dice', is also possible. In that case the image is of words randomly scattered on the word-heath – the *campus rhetorum* or *verborum* is a classical metaphor for the orator's sphere of activity – like so many dice rolling in all directions over the gaming-board.

An inept, obscure style is no match for Hartmann's crystalline words. Therefore it is impertinent, suggests Gottfried, of the hare's companion to lay claim to Hartmann's laurels. Anyone who does so must first have his flowers, the ornaments of his style, judged by his colleagues. 'We want to be in on the election too; we, who help to gather the flowers which are woven into that garland of acclaim, want to know what he is after. Let whosoever desires the laurels step forward and offer his flowers for inspection. By his flowers we shall judge whether they suit the laurels so well that we should transfer them from Hartmann to him' (4645–55). This is not the straightforward defence of Hartmann's right to the laurels that it may appear to be. Gottfried has, after all, succeeded in planting in the minds of his audience the idea that the laurels can be taken away from one poet and given to another if his 'flowers' are judged to be of superior quality; thus, subtly, Gottfried announces his own challenge to Hartmann's supremacy on the German Parnassus.

(5) *Reiteration of the question* (4821–5). Gottfried remembers that he is digressing from the task in hand; 'Tristan is still unprepared for his accolade'.

(6) *Reiteration of embarrassment* (4826–58). Again Gottfried emphasizes his inability to prepare Tristan adequately; 'I do not know how I am to prepare him' (4826). His review of other writers and their eloquence has reinforced his own sense of inadequacy; his intellect and his tongue are paralysed.

(7) *Divine machinery* (4859–964). As a way out of his embarrassment, Gottfried considers something he has never done before: praying to the Muses for a drop of inspiration from their spring. If he can obtain this, his intellect and his tongue will be restored, his words will be refined in a crucible like Arabian gold, and his eloquence, walking upon a path of clover and flowers from which every last speck of dust has been removed, will cast shade for every heart with its greenest linden-leaves. The invocation to the Muses, a highly literary device with a tradition reaching back to Homer, affords Gottfried an opportunity to show off his facility with the divine machinery of Homeric and Virgilian epic, the assemblage of deities and supernatural beings involved in the narrative of human affairs. Along with the Muses Gottfried mentions Apollo, the Sirens, and the Camenae (the latter were spring deities who, like the Sirens, were often identified with the Muses). Helicon is twice named as the address to which the request is to be sent, first as the home of Apollo and the Muses (4865–72), then as 'true Helicon', the location of the supreme throne and the heavenly choirs (4897–906). Whether Apollo's Helicon and this second, 'true' Helicon are one and the same has been the cause of some debate. The conflation of pagan and Christian mythology is not unusual by twelfth-century standards; the Muses and the angelic choirs were readily associated because in both cases they are nine in number. The second mention of Helicon may therefore be intended as no more than a reiteration and enhancement of the prayer to the Muses. There is, however, a long-established tradition of biblical exegesis that interprets persons, things and deeds in the Old Testament as prefigurations or 'types' of their counterparts or 'antitypes' in the New; the antitype is regularly designated by the epithets *novus* ('new') or *verus* ('true'). Thus, for instance, Eve is a type of Mary, the 'new' or 'true' Eve who supersedes the old. 'True Helicon' may therefore be intended by Gottfried as a typological signal: now he will cease to invoke the pagan Muses and instead direct his entreaty to the supreme and true source of inspiration, the Holy Spirit. Prayers to the Holy Spirit are conventional in Christian poetry, Latin and vernacular. More

important, to my mind, than the question whether Gottfried considered the ultimate source of poetic inspiration to reside with the Holy Spirit is the fact that he has exploited typology to show that he knows not one, but *two* ways of writing a prayer for inspiration. They are two more literary models in addition to all the other ones he has demonstrated he can handle with aplomb.

There is a further reason why it does not matter a great deal who the ultimate addressee of Gottfried's prayer may be: the prayer is never actually sent. It remains a suggestion, something that Gottfried considers he might do, but does not. This part of the excursus abounds in modal constructions, subjunctives and conditionals, which create an air of potentiality and intentionality. 'I do not know what I am to do, unless I were to do the one thing that truly I have never done before. For the first time I will send my prayer and my entreaty [...] up to Helicon [...] and if I can obtain [a drop of the Muses' inspiration] I will be able to hold my own in matters of eloquence. Indeed that same single drop is never so small that it would fail to put right and straight my tongue and my intellect' (4859–87). In spite of the benefits he can expect, Gottfried decides not to go ahead with his prayer. 'Supposing now that I were granted all the words I have requested, that I had a treasury of eloquence at my disposal, sweetened my words for everyone's ears, cast shade for every heart with the greenest linden-leaves, trod an even path with my eloquence, clearing and cleaning it with every step [...] so that it walked upon nothing but clover and bright flowers: yet I will not apply what slight intellect I have to something that has been the undoing of many others who essayed the quest and the hunt. Truly, I do better to forbear' (4908–28).

The decision not to pray for inspiration is only a temporary resting-point in Gottfried's chain of speculation. He justifies his forbearance in another long conditional sentence. 'If I were to devote all my might to preparing a knight as, God knows, many a man has done, and if I told you how Vulcan [...] and my lady Cassandra [prepared Tristan] [...] how would that have any different force from the way in which I prepared Tristan's companions for his accolade earlier on?' (4929–64). The hypothetical description of how Vulcan and Cassandra between them manufacture Tristan's equipment is a highly accomplished instance of the *ministeria deorum* beloved of classical and classicizing epic: Vulcan 'the good craftsman' forges Tristan's hauberk, sword and jambs, devises his escutcheon and his helmet, surmounted with Love's fiery dart; Cassandra, 'the skilled Trojan woman', prepares his robes. Cassandra was famed as a weaver as well as a prophetess; by choosing to present her in this role, Gottfried maintains his textile imagery to the last.

(8) *Reprise of allegory* (4965–5011). Gottfried announces his final decision on what to do: since Vulcan and Cassandra cannot prepare Tristan's apparel and knightly equipment any better than the four splendours, he will commend the hero into their care. Why the long detour? The digression, set in train by the question, how shall I prepare Tristan? gives Gottfried an opportunity to demonstrate the many literary models he can execute to perfection. Feigning incapacity, he shows his resourcefulness in handling the convention of the modesty topos. Considering cures for his paralysed intellect and tongue, he leaves his public in no doubt that he has a sovereign command of the divine machinery of classical epic, that he is no stranger to typology and can write prayers for Christian inspiration into the bargain. The only embarrassment that really afflicts him is *embarras de richesse*. All the while that his faculties are supposedly *hors de combat*, his powers of invention are undiminished, his eloquence coruscates, and the imagery and metaphors are stitched into a seamless whole. Gottfried is the master-tailor, showing his clients his pattern-book. Or, still within his chosen field of metaphor, he puts his flowers on display in a bid for the laurels.

   Though he may praise them, Gottfried thinks he can outdo all the other poets on his German Parnassus. Hartmann, the laureate, was the author who had introduced Arthurian romance into Germany and therefore had some right to be considered the doyen of chivalric description in Gottfried's day. Yet Hartmann is bested by Gottfried: the allegory of the four

splendours and the allusion to Vulcan and Cassandra reveal
that Gottfried has not one, but two models for depicting
knightly splendour in his pattern-book. Moreover, by weaving
into his text the figure of Cassandra, who in her turn weaves the
hero's clothes, he also demonstrates that he can do better than
Bligger: here is tapestry-work that surely can hold its own
against the elaborately fringed and embroidered product of
Bligger's fairy-enchanted genius. Perhaps the most audacious
act of outdoing concerns Veldeke. In the *Eneasroman* there is a
long passage describing the preparation of the hero's knightly
equipment before he goes into battle with his enemies: Vulcan
forges Eneas' helmet, jambs, sword and shield; the goddess
Pallas competes with Arachne to weave his banner (ed. Fromm,
Frankfurt, 1992, 159,1–162,38). Gottfried's hypothetical account
of how he might have Tristan's hauberk, sword, jambs, helmet,
escutcheon and robes forged and woven by Vulcan and
Cassandra, the skilled Trojan woman, is plainly intended to
evoke Veldeke's description of the preparation of the Trojan
Eneas. Gottfried appears, then, to consider doing what all of his
literary contemporaries do, namely pick his flowers from the
tree of Veldeke's eloquence. But Gottfried ends by giving the
hero not to Vulcan and Cassandra but to the four splendours
instead. The implied message is that although he could easily
emulate Veldeke's example if he wished, he will not; that
although he might pray to the Muses to obtain inspiration like
Veldeke's (he is said by Gottfried to have drunk of the spring of
Pegasus on Mount Helicon (4730–1)), he prefers the figment of
his own, supposedly uninspired imagination to the divine
machinery of classical and classicizing epic. Gottfried wants to
do nothing less than graft his own, new twig of eloquence onto
the tree of German literature.

The preparation of Tristan by the four splendours is not the
end of the matter. If we follow Gottfried a little beyond the
allegory of the four splendours, we will see how he also outdoes
the minnesingers. When the hero has at last been made ready,
Gottfried appends the comment that although his outer clothes
are identical to those of his companions, yet he stands out from
them 'in respect of his inborn clothes, which come from the

chamber of the heart and go by the name of noble spirit' (4993–5). Alois Wolf has pointed out that Gottfried has a habit of making his decisive points in what appear to be superfluous statements (*Mythe*, p. 99); the distinctive clothing of the hero is described only now, as an afterthought. The consistent equation throughout the whole excursus of woven finery and stylistic ornament invites us to interpret Tristan's inner clothes as a metaphor for Gottfried's eloquence which, because it comes from the heart, can reveal what is in the heart. The 'noble spirit' in Tristan's heart immediately brings to mind the prologue where, it will be recalled, Gottfried presents his work to noble hearts, 'to those hearts who hold a place in my own heart, to the world into which my heart sees' (48–9). His is a poetry from the heart, of the heart, for the heart. As such it is more fitting, more agreeable, more effective by far than the song of the nightingales, which does the heart good. Gottfried's conviction that he can outdo the minnesingers as poets of the heart explains the surprisingly caustic note on which his eulogy of them ends. 'May they sing so that they bring their sorrow and their plaint of love to joy, and may I live to see this happen!' (4817–20). This valediction really means, 'I hope I will live to see the day when they finally dry up!' Gottfried, who professes to be struck dumb by other poets' eloquence, can indeed be confident that his poetry of the heart will silence not only the nightingales, but all of the poets he names in his literary gallery.

Wolf has also drawn attention to the connexions between Gottfried's excursus and troubadour lyric of the second half of the twelfth century. The poets' gallery has a precedent in a *sirventes* (polemic or invective poem) by Peire d'Alvernhe, 'I will sing of those troubadours who sing in many hues' (*Lieder*, ed. R. Zenker, Erlangen, 1900, XII); the notion that true poetry comes from the heart is expressed by Bernart de Ventadorn in a song which begins 'Singing will be to no avail if the song does not come from within the heart' (*Chansons d'amour*, ed. M. Lazar, Paris, 1966, II). To these links with the poetry of the south of France I would like to add a lyric allusion closer to home. In one of his songs the leader of Gottfried's nightingales, Walther von der Vogelweide tells his love that he prefers her to

other ladies who are noble, rich and proud, for although 'they
may be better, you are good' ('lîhte sint si bezzer, dû bist guot')
(*Gedichte*, ed. H. Kuhn, Tübingen, 1959, XXIV, 24). 'Good' is
better than 'better'. Gottfried, protesting his incapacity for the
first time, had claimed that with twelve tongues at his command
he still would not know how to say anything good ('guotes iht')
about splendour such that others had not already spoken better
('baz') (4614–15); he resigns himself finally to having the four
splendours prepare Tristan 'because it cannot be done any
better' ('sit ez niht bezzer werden kan') (4982). This apology ('I
am afraid I cannot manage anything better') is also a boast: 'My
way cannot be bettered'. The little good that Gottfried claims
he can manage on this occasion is, like Walther's lady, better
than better.

Chapter 4

Commentary and narrative

In the Arthurian romances of Chrétien, Hartmann and Wolfram the meaning of the story is bound up with its structure. The narrative is a carefully worked-out total design, and the reader who has appreciated the pattern in the plot has the key to its meaning. In the contemporary Tristan romances, including Gottfried's, the plot is comparatively unstructured. It probably grew out of the agglomeration of various story-types of Celtic tradition; the resulting whole is a linear progression of more or less loosely connected episodes, beginning with the hero's parents and ending with the lovers' death. Moving a scene from its proper place in a plot of Chrétien's devising would spoil the structure and obscure the story's meaning. The component elements of Tristan romances, by contrast, are sometimes susceptible of reshuffling without detriment to either structure or meaning. For instance, in the versions of Thomas and Gottfried, Isolde's ordeal precedes the lovers' withdrawal to the cave, whereas Beroul places it after the equivalent episode of the forest and Eilhart replaces it by a different incident altogether, the wolf-trap set by Mark to catch Tristrant. These variations in the order and the components of the narrative are accompanied by different emphases (Beroul concentrates on the public and political implications of adultery, Eilhart on private feelings of enmity and friendship, Gottfried on the psychology of doubt); the variety of perspectives has more to do, however, with narrative mode than narrative structure.

The meaning of Gottfried's work will not be unlocked by the analysis of its plot; indeed it may be impossible to reduce a story as episodic as that of Tristan and Isolde to a clear structural schema of the kind that can be abstracted from the plots of Arthurian romances. Mindful of this difficulty, the critical quest for meaning in Gottfried has gone down a different path.

A distinctive feature of Gottfried's technique is the constant weaving into the narrative of authorial commentary. It is here, in the author's reflexions on the story he is telling, that readers have hoped to find the key to understanding the work.

The size and the scope of Gottfried's commentaries vary. There are pithy, gnomic sayings and there are discursive passages running to several hundred lines. Some commentaries are simple aphorisms on the way of the world: 'The affairs of men very often turn to ill fortune and from ill fortune back again to good' (1865–8). Others give practical advice: 'A man should choose the lesser of two evils; that is a useful precept' (7320–2). Others again theorize the psychology of lovers: 'It is hard to refrain from what lies sealed and locked in our hearts all the time; we are eager to do what preys upon our thoughts' (17817–21). Underlying all this variety of commentary is the same principle of generalization from specifics. A particular event or circumstance – in our examples the death of Tristan's parents, his decision to risk the voyage to Ireland, the restrictions placed on him and Isolde at court – is the pretext for setting forth some general rule or proposition. It is the principle that we saw at work in Thomas' excursus on 'estrange amor' (above, pp. 39–40). Generalization from specifics was a widespread rhetorical procedure. Rhetoric classed questions for debate as either definite or indefinite. Definite questions (*quaestiones finitae*) concern specific facts, people, times and places; they are concrete, individual and practical. Indefinite questions (*quaestiones infinitae*) have no specific reference, being abstract, general and theoretical. Quintilian illustrates the difference neatly: 'Should Cato marry?' is a definite question, 'Should a man marry?' indefinite (*Institutio oratoria*, III.5.8). Strictly speaking, the orator deals only with the first kind of question; indefinite questions are the business of philosophers. Yet how is the orator to determine whether Cato should marry without also considering the desirability of marriage for men in general? Because the narrow question cannot be answered apart from the broader one, from which it is in fact derived, the orator must attend to whatever theoretical principles are raised by the definite issue in hand in order to amplify and clarify it.

Gottfried's generalizations similarly aim at amplification and clarification of the story. He suspends the narrative to adduce general principles, then demonstrates their relevance to the particular case, typically by leading back into the story with a phrase of the kind 'thus it was with such-and-such a person' or 'thus it was in such-and-such a situation'.

There is no consensus of critical opinion about how exactly Gottfried's *ex cathedra* remarks and theoretical disquisitions are related to his narrative, and in particular to the lovers Tristan and Isolde. Does the commentary draw out a doctrine of love from their exemplary practice, or is its purpose to put a distance between the ideal of love and the actual conduct of the lovers, which is shown up for being less than exemplary? What kind of theoretical gloss on the narrative, positive, negative or ironical, is provided by the commentary turns out in fact to be a question of the second order; the fundamental problem is whether the commentary articulates any coherent ideology at all. Gottfried's practice of generalizing from changing specifics often results in commentary that is, to borrow a term from Winfried Christ, 'microstructural'; its explanatory power is restricted to a particular incident or a character's behaviour in certain quite specific circumstances. I do not think, however, that all Gottfried's commentary is microstructural. Some of it is clearly 'macrostructural', developing categories that offer the reader a consistent perspective on Gottfried's entire project. In my opinion this perspective does not consist chiefly in a doctrine of love nor indeed in any philosophy or outlook; rather it concerns the way in which an idea of love, as oneness and mutuality, may be mediated in literature.

Microstructures: commentary and character

As an example of microstructural commentary let us examine one excursus. Its theme is doubt and suspicion in love. The excursus is preceded by a summary of the narrative situation. Mark, suspecting that Tristan and Isolde are lovers but lacking proof, is plagued by doubt (13749–76). Now Gottfried starts his commentary, by posing two questions. 'What indeed can be more harmful to love than doubt and suspicion? What oppresses the amorous spirit so sorely as doubt?' (13777–80). With these questions the discourse changes gear from definite to indefinite. Gottfried no longer narrates the predicament of an individual, Mark, but discusses an abstract type. The amorous spirit is afflicted by chronic uncertainty: just when it thinks it can lay its doubts to rest, something turns up to rekindle them (13781–90). It is great folly to entertain doubt in love, but everyone does (13791–6). A worse crime against love, however, is committed whenever doubt is reduced to certainty. A lover who succeeds in confirming his suspicion exposes his heart to grief beyond all sorrow; he would gladly revert to his former state of uncertainty, if he could, for doubt and suspicion now seem good to him by comparison with the greater evil of certainty (13797–820). Thus the questions that set the excursus in train are answered. Doubt is inevitable in love, which can survive suspicion, but not the harm done by the truth when it is discovered (13821–8). Yet love is evidently her own worst enemy for, Gottfried continues, it is her habit never to stay with a satisfactory status quo, but to fasten on to doubts and suspicions and pursue them until certain heartbreak (13829–42). Then Gottfried returns to the story: 'Mark too followed tenaciously this same senseless habit' (13843–4); he is bent on resolving his doubts into certainty that will grieve his heart (13845–52). There follows the account of his bedtime dialogues with his wife, whom he hopes to trick into divulging the truth.

The excursus recasts the initial narrative situation, that of Mark beset by doubt and suspicion, as an instance of the universal condition of lovers. The king, a definite person, has become a function of an indefinite type. Likewise the policy he subsequently adopts for finding out the truth is shown to be in accordance with love's habitual way of operating. The behaviour of an individual is derived from general principles, which render it intelligible and enable one to predict its development and final outcome. Karl Bertau has remarked that Gottfried's characters are 'Marionetten des Kommentars' (*Deutsche Literatur*, p. 930), and to the extent that Mark is reduced by this excursus to a function of a type, it might indeed be said of him that he has become a puppet of the author's commentary. There remains, however, something in this digression that is surplus to the requirement of explaining the definite by derivation from the indefinite. Gottfried's reasoning implies advice: if doubt is folly, then lovers should avoid it; as the lesser of two evils it is nevertheless preferable to certainty. Yet the advice applies to a class of persons who have no choice in the matter: 'There's no getting round it for anyone: love is inevitably the mother of doubt' (13821–2); moreover, love is not in the habit of leaving doubts to slumber. To love is to doubt, it seems, and the lover inevitably progresses from doubt to certainty. Mark may be foolish, he may be embarked on a course that will end in certain grief and shatter his love for Isolde, but neither he nor any lover can act otherwise. When he discovers the lovers in the orchard Gottfried is provoked to comment, 'Truly, though, it is my belief he would have been happier believing than knowing' (18225–7). This is not advice, but sarcasm, rendered all the more pungent by the author's smug assertion that it is his belief, not his certain knowledge, that Mark would have done better to stay uncertain. Detached from any sort of practicality, Gottfried's argument – the folly of doubt is actually good, certainty is worse than uncertainty – becomes a display of sophistry for its own sake. It is, in the description of Winfried Christ, whose very fine analysis of this excursus I have made my own in these paragraphs, 'Klugrederei' (*Rhetorik und Roman*, p. 60), a piece of clever talk in which, as in the literary excursus, the author holds up his own ingenuity and intellectual superiority to wonder.

Although it is couched in the terms of a *quaestio infinita*, the excursus has only intermittent validity. Its supposedly universal principles do not govern Mark's doubt for all of the time, and they are even contradicted by what Gottfried says in another excursus. The later episode of the lovers' banishment from court and their withdrawal to the cave is introduced by an account of how their demeanour fuels the king's suspicion until, overwhelmed by anger, he 'quite forgot doubt and suspicion [...] he did not care in the slightest whether it was lies or the truth' (16513–34). Here Mark has broken out of love's habit,

that infernal addiction of pursuing doubts which was supposed
to propel him inexorably to the truth; his action is guided now
by his anger, which induces an indifference to truth and
falsehood which Gottfried calls 'blind anguish' (16535). The
themes of doubt and blindness are discussed again when the
lovers have returned to court. Mark 'the doubter' is sure at last
that Isolde loves Tristan and not him. Yet, in spite of the earlier
assertion that certainty spells the death of love, he still loves her
(17712–37). Gottfried explains this state of affairs, which is the
exact opposite of what the excursus on doubt and suspicion led
us to expect, in another commentary. Love, he says, is
proverbially blind; the lover denies the evidence of his eyes and
his intellect. 'Thus it fared with Mark: he knew as sure as death
and saw plainly that his wife Isolde loved Tristan with all her
heart and all her senses; yet he did not want to know it'
(17746–52). If love is blind, Gottfried's invoking of the adage is,
at the very least, short-sighted, for it directly contradicts the
earlier excursus on doubt and suspicion. Then love was
inveterately suspicious, and all lovers impelled by a destructive
will to knowledge; now love is proverbially blind, and lovers
universally possessed by the desire not to know.

The same short-sightedness attends Gottfried's advice on
continence. He narrates on one occasion that whenever Tristan
and Isolde were prevented from being together, they made do
with the will in place of the fact (16411–13). From their example
is derived a rule of conduct for all lovers: since the mere thought
of what is desired gladdens and enlivens the heart, a lover in
unpropitious circumstances 'should take the will in place of the
deed' (16426). Now, given the availability of this simple and
satisfying means for coping with obstacles to the realization of
passion, it is puzzling that Tristan does not follow the advice at
other times when it would have been appropriate, for instance
on the night when flour has been strewn between his bed and
Isolde's. Then the maxim that guides him is 'Love should have
no eyes, and knows no fear when she is in earnest' (15166–8).
On the one hand, then, it is posited that lovers are rational
beings, capable of estimating risks and choosing the wisest
course of action; on the other they are fearless and blind to all

danger. True, when he has noticed the flour on the floor, 'love's blind man' Tristan does consider a choice: whether to walk across to Isolde or to jump (15179–86).

Gottfried coins indefinite principles for the nonce, without much regard, it seems, for what is said or done on other occasions. It is impossible to found any consistent psychology on the shifting postulates of his ad hoc theorizing, which assumes that lovers are now rational, now blind, now addicted to uncovering the truth, now thrall to their illusions. The inconsistency of the commentary rubs off on the characters whose thoughts and deeds it is intended to explain. Although their behaviour in any single episode may be consistent with the principles expounded there, over the length of the narrative the protagonists appear as a succession of contradictory types. Mark is first a suspicious then an ignorant-but-contented husband; Tristan is a reckless lover in one scene, a calculating adulterer in another. Making the characters puppets of contradictory psychological postulates exacerbates an already existing problem of characterization in the work. The protagonists are not portrayed in a way that makes it easy to gain any hold on them as personalities defined by a steady core of character traits. The Isolde whom the prologue asks us to admire as a paragon of loyal purity (231) is also the murderous queen who plots in secret to kill Brangaene (12723, 12873). Mark, the stern upholder of patriarchal morals who can be counted upon to have his own sister put to death or, at the very least, disinherited for bearing an illegitimate child (1470–81), degenerates into a vacillating cuckold, unable to take effective measures against his wife's adultery. As to Tristan, he so often disguises his identity that one wonders whether he is less a character than a collection of aliases. To the pilgrims he encounters shortly after the Norwegians have abandoned him in Cornwall he pretends to be a native of those parts who has lost his way out hunting (2695–701); shortly after that he tells Mark's courtiers that he is a merchant's son from Parmenie (3097–9); in Ireland he assumes the guise of Tantris, a merchant from Normandy (8796–804); to Isolde's abductor Gandin he pretends to be a fellow Irishman (13301–3).

The inconsistency of commentary and character alike has been put down to Gottfried's technique of 'rhetorical particularism' (Christ, p. 117). The author concentrates on embellishing single episodes without regard to the coherence of the whole. Tristan himself is a faithful reflexion of his creator's procedure: the various stories he invents about himself contradict one another, but each is plausible in itself and is believed by his interlocutors, whoever they are at the time. The result of rhetorical particularism, of saying whatever carries conviction at the moment when it is said, is that the work becomes an aggregate of microstructures, of episodes and passages consistent in themselves, but not integrated into a larger whole. The piecemeal quality of Gottfried's work is reinforced by the fact that more than one literary genre has played a part in its making. It has long been recognized that the episodes in which Tristan and Isolde deceive Mark by their cunning have parallels in the fabliau, a medieval genre of short, amusing tales in verse where stories of how adulterers dupe a suspicious husband are legion. The guile of the lovers in these episodes – which has perplexed many of Gottfried's commentators, so out of keeping is it with his promotion of the lovers' exemplarity – reflects not on their character, but on the generic affiliations of the scenario they are currently acting out. Similarly Isolde's plot to murder Brangaene is a variation on a traditional story-motif, that of the substitute bride. In stories of this type a servant stands in for her mistress on her wedding-night so that the husband will not notice that his wife is no virgin. The mistress fears that she will be permanently supplanted by her servant, and plots to eliminate her. Isolde's uncharacteristic cruelty towards Brangaene is, then, the result of her performing the role demanded of her by the scenario. Gottfried's characters are, in fact, doubly puppets: of the author's variable commentary, and of whatever genre conventions obtain in any single episode.

Recognizing Gottfried's rhetorical particularism and the variety of generic influences enables us to see the work as a series of episodic microstructures. The merit of this approach lies in its encouraging us to waste no effort in attempting to reconcile irreconcilables. Its danger, on the other hand, is that it may lead us not to expect any sort of larger coherence from the text. To assume that consistency is entirely microstructural in Gottfried's writing, with each episode an island unto itself, disposes of the problem of macrostructural coherence by declaring that for the medieval author and his public it simply did not exist. They supposedly focused their attention on what they had in front of them, with no thought of how it fitted into the whole. That hypothesis is at best only partly true. Exclusive concentration on the immediate present is notoriously a feature of orality; for the listeners in Gottfried's public, who heard maybe no more than one or two episodes at a single recital, all that may have mattered was that each scene should ring true in itself. But it is less obvious why the same argument should apply to a literate author and his readers; they can turn the pages backwards and forwards (Gottfried recommends this (8737–8)) and note inconsistencies. There are other reasons why I do not think it can safely be assumed that Gottfried and his contemporaries had no sense of continuity and consistency. The elaborate structural patterning of Arthurian romance presupposes just such a sense, which is also palpable in the reception of another contemporary narrative work, the *Nibelungenlied*. Its protagonists, like the characters of *Tristan*, are difficult to come to grips with: Kriemhild is both victim and malefactor, Hagen both villain and exemplar of heroic probity. One early thirteenth-century redation of the *Nibelungenlied* irons out the inconsistencies by portraying Kriemhild as uniformly innocent and Hagen as invariably wicked. That Gottfried did not similarly remove or at least mitigate the most flagrant inconsistencies of characterization (I leave aside the possibility that he planned to at a later stage, and merely note that the portions of the narrative that he did complete have a 'finished' feel about them) suggests to me not that he was blind to their presence in the text, but that he had no interest in developing either the characters or their psychology into the macrostructures that could give the whole work its meaning. That does not mean that we should not look for these macrostructures elsewhere.

Macrostructures: commentary and the literary process

Much of Gottfried's commentary on the characters and their psychology is microstructural. Short-sighted, it aims no further than to illuminate the motives from which they act at any one time; it makes no contribution to a greater whole, such as the consistent portrayal of character throughout the work or the elaboration of a set of principles that could be applied to the behaviour of all lovers everywhere. But there is also commentary that is macrostructural. It too has an anchoring in the immediate narrative situation, but because it also refers to and develops what has been said before, it has validity beyond the definite episode. I am thinking above all of the 'Short Discourse on Love', the lovers' cave, and the excursus on surveillance and prohibition. These three commentaries have a common relation to the narrative. Each accompanies a depiction of the physical togetherness of the lovers in a secluded place. The 'Short Discourse' is occasioned by their first night of love-making on board the ship that carries them from Ireland to Cornwall; the cave is a lovers' idyll, surrounded by a pathless wilderness; the excursus on surveillance is the prelude to the last scene of love-making Gottfried will narrate, in another secluded idyll, the orchard. These are scenes in which the lovers embody most forcefully the oneness of heart that constitutes Gottfried's idea of love; here, then, the question of what meaning this idea has for the audience becomes pressing. The commentaries also have a common store of themes and imagery, which connects them not only with each other, but also with the prologue and literary excursus. These connexions will be appreciated more readily by readers than by listeners; when they are made, it emerges that all five passages interlock in a macrostructure that progressively brings the whole of Gottfried's project into view. That project is the mediation of love through literature.

The three commentaries treat love as something aesthetic as well as something physical and sexual. The fusion of the aesthetic and erotic is accomplished above all by the repeated use of the imagery of the nature-idyll. A little needs to be said about this imagery and its tradition by way of introduction to the detailed discussion of the passages. The nature-idyll is not natural at all, but idealized and stylized. It has a long literary tradition, extending unbroken from classical times to the Renaissance. The *locus amoenus*, the charming place, is always composed of a number of *amoenitates* or charms: a tree, a meadow, and a brook; birdsong, flowers and a breeze are optional extras. An example from classical Latin is this nature idyll by Petronius:

A moving plane-tree cast summer shadows, as did the laurel crowned with berries and the trembling cypresses and, all round, the shorn pines with their swaying tops. Between them played a foamy brook with its wandering currents, and with its plaintive water it worried the pebbles. The place is worthy of love; a witness to this is the woodland nightingale and the town-dwelling swallow which, flitting around the grass and the sweet violets, graced the countryside with their song.

(*Satyricon*, ed. F. Buecheler, Berlin, 1922, 131)

From this evocation of nature, which contains all the *amoenitates*, it will be seen that it is also usual to emphasize the sensual delight offered by the landscape to eye and ear, and to associate the *locus amoenus* with love. By the twelfth century this manner of describing an ideal landscape had been canonized in manuals of poetics. The *Ars versificatoria*, for instance, a handbook written by Matthew of Vendome at some time before 1175, contains an elaborate description of a *locus amoenus*, which is intended to provide the would-be poet with a model for imitation (ed. F. Munari, Rome, 1988, pp. 116–26). How the Middle Ages continued the classical tradition in actual poetic practice could be illustrated by any number of examples; here is one, from the *Carmina Burana* (ed. A. Hilka and O. Schumann, vol. I, part 2, Heidelberg, 1941, no. 145):

The Muse comes with a song; let us sing likewise with sweet modulation. See how everything is turning green, meadows, countryside and grove.

The lark sings early in the morning, the thrush croaks, at nature's bidding the nightingale laments its former loss.

Now the swallow warbles, sweetly the swan sings, recalling fate, the cuckoo calls through the green woodland.

The birds sing beautifully; the earth's face is resplendent with many colours and is dissolved into its offspring, sweetly fragrant.

The lime-tree spreads wide its fronds, branches and leaves; beneath it grows thyme in the green grass where a chorus dances.

A joyfully babbling stream is seen running through the grass; the place is full of festivity. A mild seasonable wind murmurs.

The imagery of the *locus amoenus* is everywhere in Gottfried. An instance is the idyllic Maytime setting of Mark's festival, when Riwalin and Blanscheflur fall in love: 'The little woodland birds, whose purpose is to delight the ears, flowers, grass, leaves and blossom and whatever pleases the eye – the summer meadow was filled with it all. There one found every gift of May one might wish for, shade beside sunshine, the lime-tree beside the brook, soft gentle breezes' (549–59). This imagery is not confined to landscape description; in the literary excursus Gottfried uses it to convey the ideal of an elegant, cultivated, pleasurable style. Inspired eloquence is a shady branch of green linden-leaves, its path a bed of clover and bright flowers (4913–22). By contrast the unpleasurable style of the hare's companion and other inventors of wild stories bears as much shade as a stick (4673). We must keep in mind this association of the traditional imagery of the *locus amoenus* with both the idea of love and the ideal literary style as we examine each of the three commentaries in turn.

The 'Short Discourse on Love'

Tristan and Isolde have drunk the potion, declared their love, and taken Brangaene into their confidence. At this point, when the lovers are free at last to consummate their passion, Gottfried interrupts the narrative with an excursus. It takes its name from the quatrain that introduces it: 'A long discourse on love is wearisome to courtly minds; a short discourse on good love does good minds good ['kurz rede von guoten minnen / diu guotet guoten sinnen']' (12183–6). The repetition of *guot* harks back to the prologue: to the need to remember what is good, and to the recommendation of the story as a school of virtue, inwardly good for noble hearts. There is also a connexion with the literary excursus. The concern here to produce discourse ('rede') appropriate to the audience replicates Gottfried's worry there about how to make his speaking ('sprechen') pleasing and apt (4591–6). The attentive readers (and perhaps listeners) who have picked up the cross-references will expect a resumption of the discussion of what relevance the love-story and Gottfried's eloquence have for them.

The 'Short Discourse' is a vituperative blast against contemporary morals. The object of Gottfried's censure, in which he includes himself, is 'we false lovers, love's deceivers' (12311–12). The picture he paints of present abuses, of the corruption and venality of love, contrasts forcefully with the ideal embodied by Tristan and Isolde in the past. It is their contentedness, which Gottfried says he can intuit, even though he has little personal experience of love's sweet suffering, that starts off the comparison between past and present: 'I have thought much about the two of them and remember ['gedenke'] today and every day. Whenever I unfold love and her plaint of desire before my eyes and meditate in my heart upon their nature, my thoughts wax and so does my companion, the spirit, as though he would soar into the clouds' (12200–08). *Gedenken* is another key word of the prologue. Gottfried puts himself here in the situation of a recipient of his story, describing its inspiriting effect on him; like the eucharistic communicant he is uplifted in heart and soul. Elation turns to pity, however, as soon as he brings back to mind present reality: 'And I take pity on love with all my soul, that most people alive are devotees and adherents of love, yet nobody among them does her justice' (12217–21).

Now Gottfried changes person from confessional 'I' to preacher's 'we'. (The excursus is sometimes known by the alternative name of 'Minnebußpredigt', because in rhetoric and tone it resembles a penitential sermon.) Like a preacher, Gottfried takes his text from the Bible. 'Whatsoever a man soweth, that shall he also reap' (Galatians 6: 7). We false lovers sow seeds of henbane (12228) in the hope that they will flower into lilies and roses (another biblical image, this time Song of

Solomon 2: 1: 'I am the rose of Sharon, and the lily of the valleys'). The metaphors are explained: henbane stands for falsehood and deceit, their harvest is disgrace and suffering (12239, 12252); roses and lilies are the desired crop of pleasure in body and heart (12240–1). When we reap the iniquity we have sown, we blame not ourselves, but love. Gottfried rounds off the exposition of his text by drawing the lesson: let us resolve to sow better seed in the future, and prepare the ground (12278) for a harvest of what we desire, 'a lover's constancy [...] which bears roses among thorns' (12269–71).

The false love of Gottfried's day and age bears 'iniquity, evil fruit and an evil crop' (12243); true love, which everyone desires and Tristan and Isolde exemplify, is a delightful garden of roses and lilies. We are familiar with this contrast, between the *locus amoenus* and its counter-image of inhospitable barrenness, from the literary excursus; there, however, the contrastive imagery expresses not different kinds of loving, but different styles of writing, the cultivated and elegant versus the barbarous and unpleasurable. Good writing is like good loving, a *locus amoenus* of sweet-smelling flowers. The similarity of the two things allows scope for a sort of homoeopathic magic: perhaps the cultivation and appreciation of fine writing, such as Gottfried's, can make the garden of our poisoned love flower again. That would accord with the prologue's recommendation of the love-story as a school of virtue, to which the word *guot* in the opening quatrain of the 'Short Discourse' alluded. But in the prologue, it will be recalled, Gottfried pulled the rug from under his programme of moral fortification. He stated that very few people (or maybe no people) in his day and age strive for heartfelt love; in the prologue's final, eucharistic, model of literary reception there is a strong suggestion that the flame of true love is rekindled in the experience of fiction alone. In the 'Short Discourse' Gottfried takes up this question again. Having admonished his fellows to sow better in future (which suggests that a real improvement in present morals can be achieved through a collective pulling up of socks), he reasons that we can be encouraged in our good intentions by stories of lovers from the past. 'Fine stories about amorous matters' and 'discourse about those who lived formerly, many hundreds of years ago' (12320–4) bring such cheer to our hearts 'that there is scarcely anyone loyal and true, and without guile towards his lover, who would not want to create the same pleasure in his own heart for himself' (12327–32). It seems that we can realize the example set by lovers in the past, about whom we learn from literature, in our own conduct. But there is a condition: whoever sets out to do this must first be 'loyal and true, and without guile towards his lover'. There are no such people in the world nowadays, says Gottfried, who continues, 'The one thing, though, from which everything grows up lies piteously all the time beneath our feet: that is loyalty, which comes from the heart' (12333–6). This is a demolition of optimism more complete than that performed in the prologue, which at least kept alive the hope that there still were a few steadfast lovers in the world. Of the true love of the past, such as that being consummated even as Gottfried speaks by Tristan and Isolde, there remain to us, as to Gottfried at the beginning of this discourse, only the intuition and inspiriting remembrance. The ideal of good loving cannot be experienced except in the literary imagination; the only *locus amoenus* we can hope to inhabit is the well-tended garden of Gottfried's style.

The 'Short Discourse' removes the fact of true love to an irrecuperable past; all that present-day lovers have of it is fine tales and words, 'schœne mære' and 'rede'. To love in the present is to be a connoisseur of a cultivated, pleasurable style, an elite taster of the sweet bread of Gottfried's literary eucharist. This reinforces my earlier suggestion that the term 'noble heart' may designate not a group of recipients who are exemplary in virtue of the love they practise, but the affective state produced in those readers and listeners who open their hearts to Gottfried's 'senemære', his tale of desire, and his 'rede', his words, his eloquence. It is in the encounter with words that noble hearts are called to life and the ideal of love is made real again.

The 'Short Discourse on Love' is to the narrative of the lovers' physical union as Gottfried's entire work of verbal art is to the ideal it represents: words in place of the fact of love. The

'Short Discourse' is words in place of the sex act between the lovers Tristan and Isolde, over which Gottfried prefers to draw the decorous veil of his eloquence. Indeed, this veiling, this movement from act to words, starts before the discourse proper, when it is narrated how love, personified first as physician then as ensnarer, joined Tristan and Isolde together in an indissoluble bond (12160–82). The allegory is a euphemism for sexual intercourse; it is also a literary game. The personification of love as physician is another example, alongside the prologue's recommendation of love stories as comfort for suffering lovers, of how Gottfried turns Ovid's *Remedia amoris* against him. Ovid presents himself throughout this poem as a physician whose medicine will cure the lover of his complaint; in Gottfried the supreme healer is the malady itself. The hunting metaphor is also from Ovid; we remarked earlier (p. 28) that Gottfried plays with the two senses of MHG *strickærinne*, 'ensnarer' and 'binder', to transform the negative image of being trapped in love's toils into the positive one of an everlasting bond reminiscent of marriage. The narrative of the lovers' first union climaxes, then, in a play with literary and religious language. Words, not deeds, have become the object of the poet's attention.

Word-play holds a danger. In his invective against our present corruption, Gottfried laments that we have driven love to the remotest corner of the earth, keeping only her name; 'and we have worn even that so thin, so overused and abused the word and the name ['also zetriben, also verwortet und vernamet'], that she, poor tired creature, is ashamed of her own name' (12284–7). The verbs *verworten* and *vernamen*, neologisms of Gottfried's, are extremely difficult to translate. They can mean 'to abuse a word, name'; the sense of the author's lament is, then, that nowadays we call by love's name all manner of venality and fraud, crimes against which he inveighs a few lines later (12300–10). Since, however, the verbs are in collocation with *zetrîben*, they could also mean 'to wear away by overuse', which adds a new undertone to the complaint: too much love-talk makes the word trite. Corruption, attrition, trivialization of love's name – all these dangers also attend

Gottfried's own discourse, which is words about love for a world where the reality is missing. Perhaps the risk can be averted by keeping one's words pure, crystalline and well washed, and the path of one's discourse free from every speck of dust. These are all virtues of eloquence that Gottfried admires and wishes for in the literary excursus (4628–9, 4660, 4915–20).

The narrative itself provides an example of how the truth of love is conveyed by a well-washed word. Like Gottfried and his contemporaries, Tristan and Isolde also play with the word 'love', treating it as an object. Falling in love is easy for them; finding words to avow their passion gives difficulty. Isolde resorts to the device of complaining that she is afflicted by 'lameir' (11986–8), leaving it to Tristan to determine which of the three possible meanings, the sea, bitterness, love, she intends. In Gottfried this process becomes a more artificial game than in Thomas because it is based on a foreign word, whose meaning has to be glossed for German-speakers (11994–5). To them 'lameir' is verbal matter, almost an object that can be handled. Tristan's own interpretative handling of it is a sort of *verworten*, a wearing down of the word's meaning, but unlike the corrupting activity Gottfried decries among his contemporaries, his *verworten* reduces the word to its truth, the fact of the love between him and Isolde. Tristan's guessing-game can also be understood through one of Gottfried's positive metaphors for handling words. It is a cleaning of the word, a washing away of its irrelevant meanings to reveal its truth. The well-washed word for love brings him and Isolde a step closer to the act; Gottfried's immaculate language guarantees an efficacious representation of the love that was realized in the flesh in the past.

The Cave of Lovers

The path of Gottfried's eloquence is nowhere smoother, cleaner or greener than in the cave of lovers. The episode, one of the high points of the work, contains a series of commentaries twisted into the narrative. Its pace is measured and stately and, as a summary of its structure shows, the *locus amoenus* runs through it like a refrain.

Narrative: Tristan and Isolde are banished from the court and
    make their way to the cave (16455–688)
        The place I: description of the cave (16689–729) and
        locus amoenus (16730–66)
Narrative: the lovers arrive at the cave (16767–806)
    wunschleben I: the lovers' self-sufficiency (16807–80, 16896–908)
    in the
        locus amoenus (16881–908)
    Autobiography I (16909–22)
        The place II: allegorical exegesis of the cave (16923–17099)
    Autobiography II (17100–38)
    wunschleben II: the lovers' occupation in the cave and
        locus amoenus (17139–274)
Narrative: Mark hunts the white stag (17275–346)
    wunschleben III: the lovers' perambulation through the
        locus amoenus (17347–416)
Narrative: Mark finds the lovers, is convinced of their innocence, and
    allows them to return (17417–701)

The place

Gottfried breaks off his account of the lovers' journey to the cave in order to describe their destination at length, preparing it, so to speak, for their arrival. He begins by establishing the cave's historicity and antiquity. It was hewn into the rock by giants who ruled Cornwall in pagan times, before Corineus (16688–93). Corineus is the mythical founder of Cornwall, a pseudo-historical figure who appears in Geoffrey of Monmouth's *Historia Regum Britanniae* (*c.* 1135–8) as the leader of a group of fugitives from Troy; Geoffrey narrates how he took part in the occupation of Britain by Aeneas' great-grandson Brutus, landing in Cornwall and driving the indigenous inhabitants, giants, into caves in the mountains (ed. Acton Griscom, London, 1929, I.12–II.5). Gottfried's reference (which he may have taken either direct from Geoffrey, or from Thomas, who for his part may have got the information from an Anglo-Norman adaptation of the *Historia*, the *Roman de Brut* of Wace) anchors the cave in British prehistory and synchronizes it roughly with the sack of Troy.

The cave is a real place. Appropriately, an enumeration of physical properties follows. The cave is round, wide, high, straight and smooth; its floor is of green marble; in the middle stands a crystal bed, into which is cut a dedicatory inscription to the goddess Love; the cave has three windows, and a door of bronze (16703–29). Next comes a description of the landscape in which the cave is situated. It is a confection of all the elements of the conventional *locus amoenus*. Three lime-trees shade the cave's entrance with their branches; the surrounding mountainside is screened by countless other trees; there is a meadow through which runs a babbling spring, which another three limes shield from sun and rain; the meadow is resplendent with grass and flowers; the whole place is filled with birdsong (16730–60). Gottfried follows literary tradition by connecting the place with love, and by emphasizing the pleasure it affords eye and ear: 'There eye and ear had their pasture and their delight' (16754–5).

The cave is a unique place in Cornwall but, because all *loci amoeni* are alike, its setting could be anywhere. This movement from definite to indefinite is continued when Gottfried resumes his account of the place with an extensive allegorical interpretation of the cave. The exegesis (which may be modelled on the allegorical interpretation of church buildings) is an 'unlocking' ('entsliezen') of the significance ('meine') contained in the cave's material properties (16923–7). Its roundness stands for the simplicity of love, its breadth for love's power, the whiteness and smoothness for love's purity, and so on. The location of the entire *locus amoenus* amid a pathless wilderness is said to signify that true love is hard to attain. There was in classical literary tradition a variant of the *locus amoenus* which locates the idyllic landscape amid wild mountain slopes and forests; a famous natural example of such a place was the Vale of Tempe near Mount Olympus, and indeed the name Tempe in classical and medieval poetry designated any *locus amoenus* in the wilderness. Behind Gottfried's description of the cave and its surroundings lies the literary Tempe motif.

The literariness of the setting is underlined by the striking similarity between the imagery deployed here and that used to describe the ideal of style in the literary excursus. There Gottfried thinks out loud about the consequences of the Muses' granting his prayer for inspiration: '[Supposing that] I made my words soft to everyone's ears and offered shade to every heart with the greenmost leaf of the linden-tree [...] and [my discourse] walked only on clover and bright flowers' (4912–22). The ideal literary style is like the nature-idyll around the cave: full of greenery and flowers to delight the senses, and planted with trees affording hospitable shade to whoever, lover or noble heart, sojourns beneath them. When the lovers arrive in the *locus amoenus* Gottfried has prepared for them, it is as though they were also setting foot in the author's own elegant writing. One might say, then, that the episode of the cave celebrates the passing of the lovers into the literary tradition that will preserve their names for posterity.

wunschleben

The lovers lead a perfect life or 'wunschleben' (16846, 16872), free from material and social needs. They have no need of bodily food: all the sustenance they require is provided by thoughts, love and loyalty; these, Gottfried maintains, are their best nourishment (16807–46). Nor have they need of society: their own company was enough for them and they would not have exchanged it for Arthur and his court – the acme of social life in conventional chivalric romances. Their household is provided by the *locus amoenus* and their festival by love, who brings Arthur's Round Table to them a thousand times each day (16847–901). Gottfried sums up the portrait of self-sufficiency with the assertion that the lovers had each other, and that was all they needed: 'There man was with woman and woman with man: what more did they need? They had what they ought to have, and were where they wanted to be' (16904–8). The evocation of the lovers' self-sufficient, perfect life in an idyllic natural setting recalls the Garden of Eden: 'And the Lord God planted a garden eastward in Eden; and there he put the man whom he had formed. And out of the ground made the Lord God to grow every tree that is pleasant to the sight, and good for food [...] And a river went out of Eden to water the garden [...] And out of the ground the Lord God formed every beast of the field, and every fowl of the air [...] And the rib, which the Lord God had taken from man, made he a woman, and brought her to the man' (Genesis 2: 8–22). Eden is the archetypal *locus amoenus*, and it was not unusual for Christian poets to use the conventional *amoenitates* in order to describe paradise. Gottfried has located Tristan and Isolde, man and woman, in a latter-day Eden.

Having moved the lovers into a nature-idyll that resembles his ideal of style, it is logical that Gottfried should take the step of depicting them in a way that resembles the addressees of his style. The lovers are affected by their surroundings as noble hearts are affected by an elegant literary style: they experience sensual delight. The song of the calander-lark and the nightingale enraptures them; the murmuring brook echoes sweetly in their ears; the trees and the breeze delight their eyes and senses; flowers and grass smile at them, and the dew cools their feet and refreshes their hearts (17354–93). Compare the setting described by Gottfried in the literary excursus: there are nightingales (the minnesingers); the spring of Pegasus, which inspires Veldeke; the tree of eloquence, covered in flowers; the heath of words on which the hare's companion chases about. The likeness is appropriate, for soon Tristan and Isolde will join the ranks of the narrators and minnesingers who populate the German Parnassus.

The description of the lovers' daily occupation reinforces the resemblance between them and Gottfried's audience of noble hearts. 'In the woods and open country of their wilderness they had their leisure and their occupation ['ir muoze und ir unmuoze'] most pleasantly arranged' (17141–4). *Unmuoze* is a key word in the prologue, where the story is commended as occupation for noble hearts. The lovers' day begins with an early morning walk through the *locus amoenus*. The dewy meadow is their recreation, the stream their delight, the lime-tree's leafy shade affords them 'pleasure without and within the breast' (17147–75). This last formula, which means 'pleasure in body and heart', has been used by Gottfried before, when he describes the impact of Isolde's singing on the ears and hearts of her listeners (8051–2); it is reminiscent too of the 'pleasure of the heart' that Gottfried demands of eloquence in the literary excursus (4680). The lovers' perambulation through the charms of their Arcadian landscape is like a stroll down the path of Gottfried's well-tended style.

Seated beneath the lime-tree, Tristan and Isolde pass the time in telling each other love-stories about women who were destroyed by their desire. All of these ill-starred heroines feature in Ovid's *Heroides* and *Metamorphoses*: Phyllis hanged herself when her lover abandoned her; Canacea loved her own brother and was forced by her father to commit suicide; Biblis also loved her brother and cried herself to death when he fled her advances; Dido killed herself because Aeneas spurned her. Possibly Gottfried did not select his examples direct from Ovid, but took them out of a mythological handbook; an almost identical sequence of names appears among the list of 'women who killed themselves' in Hyginus' *Fabulae* (ed. H. J. Rose, Leiden, 1934, p. 151). Gottfried refers to the stories told by his lovers as 'senemære' (17184), the term by which he called his own narrative in the prologue. Moreover, Tristan and Isolde are occupied ('unmüezic') (17199) with these tales of desire, just as the noble hearts occupy themselves with the 'senemære' of Tristan and Isolde. There is, however, an important difference between the two audiences. Whereas Gottfried enjoined his public to remember, Tristan and Isolde are permitted to forget: 'When the two of them wanted to forget the stories, they crept into their retreat' (17200–2). Gottfried's public must not forget because, it was borne in upon them by the 'Short Discourse', they live in a world from which the reality of love has receded; remembrance, through the medium of the story, is their only access to a vanished golden age. Tristan and Isolde are by contrast still part of that age; they can set aside the tales of their predecessors because they continue them in living practice.

That practice is the next occupation to be described. Inside the cave, the lovers make music, taking turns at singing and accompanying each other on the harp (17202–17). Tongue and harp are the instruments of Bligger's fairy-enchanted eloquence (4705) – another reminiscence of Parnassus. Their harmony is so sweet 'that it was apt that the cave should be dedicated to sweet love' (17222–3). Music-making now flows effortlessly over into love-making, as though the one and the other were the same (17229–41). Both occupations reveal the essence of the cave's name and nature: 'Whatever had been told about the cave previously, in old stories, was now proven true by these two residents' (17225–8). Tristan and Isolde can fulfil old stories about love; Gottfried and his contemporaries can only have their hearts warmed by them.

The last of the occupations to be mentioned is hunting. Like music-making, hunting is a conventional metaphor for love; it is presented by Gottfried as an aesthetic pastime, like music. The lovers, he reasserts, had no need of food, hunting 'for the sake of pastime' and 'more for the pleasure it brought to their hearts and for their recreation than for food' (17264, 17268–70). As if to underline how hunting has been turned into a recreation pursued for its intrinsic pleasure, Gottfried relates how Tristan trained the dog Hiudan to hunt without barking. In the versions of Beroul and Eilhart, he does this because the dog's bark would otherwise betray him and Isolde to Mark and his court. Gottfried does not mention this reason; this training is art for art's sake. The theme of the chase provides a smooth change of scene, from the cave back to the court, where we find the king trying to dispel his melancholy through hunting.

Autobiography

If love is transformed into aesthetics in the cave and its environs, so then might aesthetic appreciation offer a form of loving to the inhabitants of Gottfried's age of iron. This seems to me to be the point of his including autobiographical commentary. Twice the author claims personal experience of the cave. The first occasion is during the discussion of food. He reassures doubters that the lovers can indeed survive without food, for he has done it himself: 'I too once led this kind of life, and I thought it was quite sufficient' (16920–2). The second autobiographical passage follows the allegorical exegesis of the cave and its landscape. Its last statement is that the cave's situation in the wilderness signifies the difficulty of finding true love; Gottfried reinforces the interpretation with another argument from personal experience: 'I know this for certain, for I was there' (17100). This time the private remark develops into a much longer digression. Gottfried narrates that he managed to penetrate the cave, opening its latch of tin and gold (the latch stands for desire and its gratification); he danced on the marble floor of steadfastness, and made his way right up to the bed, though he never lay on it. In the preceding allegory, the crystal bed symbolizes love's honesty and purity; what Gottfried is confessing is that he – like all of his contemporaries in the 'Short Discourse' – lacks the requisite qualities for true love. Thanks to the allegory, Gottfried is able to encode a personal experience of love in the metals and minerals out of which the cave is constructed, tin, gold, marble, crystal. The reader or listener who has followed and retained the details of the allegory can then decode Gottfried's account, as I have done, turning cold stone and metal back into the warm flesh and blood of erotic experience.

Whether these confessions are based in autobiographical fact is a question to which we shall never know the answer. In any case, it has no relevance for our understanding of these passages. What does matter in this respect is that the presentation of autobiographical details wavers between realism and metaphor. On the one hand, the cave is a real place; Gottfried's visit ought logically to involve an actual journey to Cornwall. On the other hand, because the topics of the *locus amoenus* and the extensive allegory impart to the cave a degree of ubiquity and generality beyond its bounded geographical existence, 'going to the cave' can also be a metaphor for experiencing love. Gottfried comes down on the side of metaphor: 'I have known the cave since I was eleven, and I have never been to Cornwall' (17136–8). Since, moreover, the cave is a confection of literary motifs and a *locus amoenus* exactly resembling the well-tended literary style, Gottfried's claim to have been visiting it from the age of eleven can mean that he has been experiencing love through literature, through the cultivation of his own writing and that of others. Eleven is not an unusual age for a medieval schoolboy to be reading Ovid and doing exercises in Latin composition.

The orchard

The last time in Gottfried's fragment when we see the lovers together is during the scenes of their assignation, discovery and parting in the orchard. Mark finds them locked in an embrace whose tightness recalls the knitting together of the lovers on their first night of passion. 'He found his wife and his nephew entwined close and tight in each other's arms, her cheek next to his, her mouth next to his [. . .] their arms and their hands, their shoulders and their chests were all pressed and locked together so tight that if it had been a statue cast in bronze or gold it could not have been better joined' (18195–211). This artwork, for that is what the lovers have become in the eyes of the king, is exhibited in a nature-idyll similar to that surrounding the cave. Gottfried narrates that Isolde 'started looking for a convenient place to lie in her orchard; she sought out a shady spot that would give her opportune shelter and help, where it would be cool and secluded. As soon as she found it, she had a bed prepared there, with great magnificence' (18139–47). The site is shaded by trees, cool and secluded; the splendid bed evokes the crystal bed in the middle of love's sanctum, the cave. The *locus amoenus* around the cave, where Tristan and Isolde wanted for nothing, resembled Eden; the lovers' meeting, discovery and parting in the orchard, which is an extension of the Arcadian scenery around the cave, will be narrated as temptation, fall and expulsion from paradise.

The Old Testament framework is made explicit in the excursus on surveillance ('huote') which precedes the lovers' assignation in the orchard. It is the last extensive commentary in Gottfried's work as it stands. In it, and in the scenes it introduces, the language and the themes of all the digressions we have been examining reappear. The starting-point for this commentary is, as with so many of Gottfried's other theoretical disquisitions, a definite narrative situation. Mark allows the lovers to return from the cave, but forbids them any display of intimacy, whether in their looks or conversation (17659–816). This specific prohibition, which is more than the lovers can bear, is the pretext for marshalling arguments against surveillance and prohibition in general. It is impossible to prevent feelings in the heart from seeking expression; prohibition makes what is forbidden appear more attractive; surveillance is wasted on women, because it will not stop the wicked ones and the good ones need no guarding anyway; whoever keeps women under surveillance sows bitterness and resentment (17817–930). In the narrative Mark's prohibition applied to both Tristan and Isolde; the commentary's narrow focus on the effects of surveillance on women alone prepares the ground for the Old Testament story of Eve. It is women's inborn nature, continues Gottfried, to do what is forbidden; in this respect they are all daughters of Eve, who would not have tempted Adam to eat the fruit of the tree of knowledge if God had not forbidden it (17931–66).

The initial relationship of commentary to narrative consists in criticism of Mark's policy: 'Wherever it is practised surveillance bears and brings forth nothing but briars and thorns' (17859–61). In returning to the imagery of the 'Short Discourse', Gottfried intimates that Mark's surveillance will poison love's garden, creating a world like that inhabited by the author and his contemporaries. The arraignment of surveillance also has an Old Testament dimension. After Adam and Eve have been expelled from Eden, God says to Adam, 'Cursed is the ground for thy sake; in sorrow shalt thou eat of it all the days of thy life; thorns and thistles shall it bring forth to thee' (Genesis 3: 17–18). Mark's prohibition will incite Isolde to tempt Tristan, and force the two of them to exchange their Arcadian paradise for a barren wilderness. The argument of the commentary sets off on a feminist tack: men do wrong to impose prohibitions on women. Accordingly, its advice is directed at men: 'Therefore a wise man, that is any man who allows woman her honour, should never offend her goodwill by subjecting her privacy to any surveillance other than guidance and instruction, gentleness and kindness' (17897–903). When, however, the example of Eve is introduced, the emphasis shifts, from male folly to female nature. Thorns, briars and thistles, the consequences of male surveillance, are now metaphors of women's inborn and hereditary insubordination: 'God knows, that same thistle and thorn are born in them; women of that kind are children of their mother Eve. She broke the first prohibition [...] and lost herself and God' (17931–46). The stock elements of clerical antifeminism raise their head, and it would be possible for Gottfried now to change tack and inveigh against the wickedness of Eve and all her sex. Instead, he implies that it is for men to make allowances for women's natural propensity to sin by not forbidding them anything; he goes so far as to insinuate that God was at fault in forbidding the fruit (17947–9). Throughout this part of the commentary it is as though Gottfried's thought struggles to resist the gravitational pull of the orthodox clerical misogyny that traditionally drew legitimacy from the example of Eve.

The change of emphasis, from castigating men to explaining female nature, allows the commentary to sustain a dual relationship with the narrative. It looks backward, to Mark's policy of surveillance, and forward, to the assignation in the orchard. Isolde appears in this scene as a latter-day Eve, transgressing the patriarchal law, represented in this case by Mark's prohibition of intimacy between her and Tristan. Like the Eve of antifeminist tradition, she is a temptress and seductress who brings about man's expulsion from paradise. Having prepared the bed in the orchard Isolde, 'the fair one, lay down on the bed wearing her shift. Then she ordered all the ladies-in-waiting to leave, except Brangaene. Now a message was despatched to Tristan, that he should not fail to speak with Isolde there and then. Now he did just as Adam had done; he accepted the fruit that his Eve offered him, and with her ate his death' (18154–64). There follows the account of the lovers' rendezvous, their discovery by Mark, their leavetaking, and Tristan's departure into exile (18165–361).

The narrative is a repetition of the Old Testament story of Adam and Eve. But against this tale of Paradise Lost, Gottfried also sets a vision of Paradise Regained. His account of female nature develops into a speculative discussion of how women might overcome Eve's legacy. A woman who succeeds in denying her nature, which always leads her to transgress the patriarchal law, is worthy of praise and admiration; she is no longer a woman except in name, for she has the mind and heart of a man (17967–85). The notion is a commonplace of Judaeo-Christian thought. In the Gnostic gospel of Mary, Jesus is magnified by Mary Magdalene: 'Praise his greatness, for he has prepared us and made us into men.' Philo of Alexandria proclaimed that 'progress is nothing else than the giving up of the female gender by changing into the male'. And Jerome, who alongside Tertullian may be considered the founding father of Christian antifeminism, asserted that a woman who leaves her husband for Jesus 'will cease to be a woman and will be called man' (cited by R. H. Bloch, *Medieval Misogyny*, Chicago, 1991, p. 107). Gottfried pushes his speculation beyond the line of antifeminist tradition. Better than the woman who, by over-coming her nature, transforms herself into a man is the one who strikes a balance between her honour and her body, in such a way as to preserve her womanly nature. This compromise is given the name 'maze', the measure or balance familiar as an ideal of courtly literature. Perfect femininity is a woman who neither wholly denies her body, nor indulges it indiscriminately. In short, it is the ideal of a woman who is faithful and constant in love (17986–18058).

Gottfried kicks against the tradition of clerical misogyny by suggesting that there might be a way for women to be good without changing their gender to the masculine. Yet his argument never gives up completely the presuppositions of the antifeminism it opposes, for it remains based on the premise that women are the weaker sex, ever ready to sin. That is as true of his discussion of Eve and the fall as it is of his speculative ideal of womanhood. His conviction that God would have done better not to forbid the fruit, outrageous though it may seem, upholds the traditional view of women's nature; the implication is that men should adjust their own behaviour in recognition of women's propensity to disobedience. Such a position is not feminism, but a species of enlightened antifeminism. The woman who has cast off Eve's legacy is neither set free from her nature nor released from the patriarchal law. She must practise sexual continence (which presupposes that she has an appetite that must be brought under control), and internalize the law. Like the good woman Gottfried mentioned at the beginning of the excursus, 'she guards herself' ('sie hüetet selbe') (17876). Gottfried's vision of ideal femininity amounts to the advocacy of a refined version of patriarchy, in which men's control of women is more subtle because it is not exercised directly, through prohibition and surveillance, but indirectly, through women's internalization of male expectations of them. It is telling that Gottfried's perfect woman must conform to his male definition of what a woman should be, and that he goes on to discuss the benefits that his speculative ideal of womanhood would bestow on men.

The man who enjoys the love of such a woman 'has living paradise planted in his heart' (18066–7). This paradise is a restored *locus amoenus*; the wilderness flowers again. 'In that place there is neither briar nor thorn; the thistle of gall has no place there at all. Rosy reconciliation has pulled it all up, thorn and thistle and briar. In this paradise nothing burgeons on the branch, nothing waxes green nor grows that the eye does not gladly see' (18073–82). It is the garden of roses and lilies that we desire to sow in the 'Short Discourse'. Gottfried concludes his speculative vision, and the entire commentary, with the suggestion that 'if any man searched, as he ought, there might be more Isoldes living ['ez lebeten noch Isolde'] in whom one could find all that one desired' (18111–14). What are we to make of the tantalizing suggestion that there are still women like Isolde to be found in the world nowadays? Does it mean that, in spite of the pessimism of the prologue and especially the 'Short Discourse', true love like that of Tristan and Isolde can yet be realized in practice? Maybe Gottfried has abandoned the line of argument he has been developing from the prologue onwards.

But there are also grounds for thinking that he is continuing it. A *locus amoenus* planted in the heart is like the style that affects the heart. Is writing the place where nowadays one should seek one's Isolde, rather as one visits the cave in the literary imagination? Anyone who believes he should seek another Isolde in reality will think differently if he follows the story as far as Tristan's exile. In Arundel Tristan too discovers that there are more Isoldes, but the entanglement with Isolde Whitehand brings him anything but the paradise of love he wishes to recreate. The phrase 'ez lebeten noch Isolde' is an ironic prediction of the rest of the narrative, warning against a naive interpretation of the injunction to seek as one ought.

Isolde, who will be depicted as a latter-day Eve in the orchard scene which follows directly on this remark, is also the prototype of the woman who has overcome Eve's legacy. In the narrative she in fact plays a double role: as Eve, whose transgression leads to the expulsion from paradise into a wilderness of thorns, and as the Isolde whose words of farewell prepare the ground for a reflowering of love in the heart. Once they have been discovered and are forced to separate, the lovers are no different from Gottfried and his contemporaries. They all live in a postlapsarian world, remote from what they desire, physical togetherness in love's garden. Like Gottfried and his noble hearts, Tristan and Isolde set about restoring their lost paradise inwardly, in their hearts and their memory. Isolde's words of farewell to Tristan in the orchard are her attempt to preserve through remembrance the paradise the lovers have just lost in actuality. She begins by calling to mind the indissoluble nature of their union. 'My lord, the devotion of our hearts and minds has been too close and too near for too long a time now for them ever to know what it may be to forget each other' (18288–93). Minutes before, when Mark had discovered the lovers, it had been their arms that were closely entwined, now it is their hearts and minds. Isolde insists on this inner togetherness as the means of keeping love alive: 'If you should ever have thoughts of loving anyone apart from me, remember ['gedenket'] then how my heart feels now. Remember ['gedenket'] this parting, how it pains us in our hearts and bodies. Remember ['gedenket'] the many sorrowful times I endured for your sake, and do not let anyone mean more to you than your beloved Isolde. Do not forget me for someone else; we two have shared joy and sorrow until now; it is right and proper that we should maintain the same devotion until death' (18310–27). Isolde's thrice repeated injunction *gedenket* is identical to the injunction to the public with which Gottfried began his prologue. Tristan and Isolde have become like Gottfried's audience, beholden to the remembrance that alone can preserve their love from oblivion. The lovers continue to exist for each other in their hearts: 'Whether you are near to me or far away, there shall be no life nor any living thing in my heart but Tristan, my self and my life' (18294–7).

By the time Isolde has finished speaking, love is no longer something a lover does, it is primarily something a lover thinks and feels, and this thinking and feeling are no less intense, no less genuine for being cultivated by one lover in the other's absence. Love has been transformed into a discourse of interiority; it has become a form of reciprocal and sentimental remembrance. Yet this remembrance cannot dispense altogether with a material basis, which consists in the ring, the kiss, and a new bodily relationship between the lovers. Ring and kiss are physical tokens of oneness without end: 'Take this ring, and let it be a token of fidelity and love [...] Now come and kiss me. Tristan and Isolde, you and I, we two are both one inseparable thing for ever. This kiss will be a seal, confirming that we shall remain each other's constantly until death, I yours and you mine, only one Tristan and one Isolde' (18307–9, 18351–8). This oneness will not be maintained without care of the body, whose importance, even in separation, is impressed upon Tristan by Isolde: 'Take care of yourself, my body ['min lip'], for if I am bereft of you, then I, who am your body ['iuwer lip'], am dead. For your sake, not mine, I will take care and good wardship ['huote'] of myself, your body ['iuwer lip'], for I know well that your body and your life ['iuwer lip und iuwer leben'] depend on me. We are one body, one life ['ein lip, ein leben']' (18336–44). When these lines were discussed earlier (pp. 36–7), *lip* was translated as 'self'. Its primary meaning is, however, 'body'. Isolde proposes that she and her lover should continue to give their bodies to each other, not now in physical lovemaking, which is what she desired when she summoned Tristan to the orchard, but by each vesting his body in the absent other, who will care for it as his own self and life. By making this proposal, which transforms love into a oneness of heart, mind *and* body in spite of physical separation, Isolde also transforms herself, from latter-day Eve to prototype of Gottfried's ideal woman. She becomes the woman who guards herself and carries off the balancing act between affirming and denying the body that Gottfried recommends. Isolde affirms her body by asking Tristan to care for it; she denies it in so far as she claims that her body is not with her, but with her lover.

Isolde's speech, and the subsequent course of the story, emphasize the permanence of the bond between the lovers. The potion joins Tristan and Isolde until death; even in separation, their love cannot cease. This is proved by Tristan's involvement with 'another Isolde'. Tristan seeks to justify his interest in her as follows: 'I have often read after all, and I know for certain, that one love takes away the force of another. The Rhine's current and stream are nowhere so great that it could not be channelled into separate currents until it abated completely and its strength became slight; thus the mighty Rhine becomes little more than a rivulet. Nor is the heat of any fire so fierce that, if one were so minded, its brands could not be dispersed until it burned but weakly. Thus it goes with a lover' (19432–48). Where has Tristan read this? In the *Remedia amoris*: 'One love takes away the force of another. Great rivers are diminished through being channelled into many streams, and a harmful flame perishes if the logs are pulled from beneath it' (444–6). Gottfried did not live to narrate Tristan's marriage to Isolde Whitehand, but if he had followed Thomas, it would have demonstrated once more the inapplicability of Ovid's cures to Gottfried's kind of lover. Tristan cannot forget Isolde by marrying her namesake.

The remainder of the plot can be reconstructed fairly reliably from Thomas and the Old Norse saga. It would have narrated Tristan's resumption of devotion to Isolde: he sets up and adores a statue of her, visits her in person, and dies for love of her. From this resumée it is plain that the form of his devotion is not confined to remembrance. Thomas relates that Tristran reminisces to Ysolt's statue (Turin[1], 1–4), but that is not all; his returns to Ysolt are in search of sexual fulfilment – in Thomas' words he 'has his pleasure with Ysolt', and the lovers 'satisfy their desire' (Douce, 723, 794). We can only speculate about what Gottfried would have made of these episodes, and about how they would have related to the position reached by the parting lovers in the orchard. It does not seem to me that they necessarily mark a relapse from spirituality into carnality. That would be putting the question in inappropriate terms. Gottfried does not oppose spiritual love to carnal love and recommend the former as the ideal; the opposition spiritual–carnal is in fact irrelevant to his work. The operative distinction is between facile pursuit of pleasure and commitment to suffering (these are the terms in which the prologue contrasts the common run of lover with the noble hearts), or between falsehood and fidelity (the two attitudes to love in the Short Discourse). The valued form of love certainly has spiritual qualities (devotion, mutuality, oneness of heart), but it is also physical love. Gottfried repeatedly emphasizes how love's spiritual virtues manifest themselves in physical things. This is true of the lovers' first night together, when the union of their hearts is symbolized in the union of their bodies; it is true of the cave, whose allegorical significance is fulfilled in the lovers' 'play'; it is true also of the excursus on surveillance, in which Gottfried commends moderation, not renunciation, of the flesh as the basis for realizing paradise on earth; and it remains true at the lovers' parting, when the continuation of their union in remembrance is founded on mutual care of the body. If this is recognized, the way is open to interpreting Tristan's subsequent exploits as continuing variations on the theme of realizing the spiritual in the flesh.

The relationship between the spiritual and the physical in Gottfried might be termed 'sacramental'. The Christian sacraments are visible signs of God's invisible grace; a material object, such as a host or wedding-ring, can function sacramentally as a token which allows the believer access to the spiritual reality he cannot see. Similarly, Gottfried's lovers achieve the spiritual virtues of fidelity, mutuality and oneness through physical lovemaking or, when they are apart, through physical acts and objects that sustain memory – care of the body, the ring and (to go by Thomas) the statue. The inner reality of love is also made accessible to the lovers who constitute Gottfried's public by means of a sacrament. This is the story, offered as bread to the noble hearts who, in tasting it, relive the pure fidelity of Tristan and Isolde. In this instance, the sacrament is clearly metaphorical; the story is not literally bread, the noble hearts do not literally taste it, and its signified content is not realized except in literary fiction. In the sweetness of Gottfried's writing the garden of love flowers anew.

Chapter 5

After Gottfried

The love of Tristan and Isolde reaches its full potential not in the life they have lived, but in literature. It flourishes in the idyll of the grotto, which is simultaneously Gottfried's bright graceful style, and it endures in memory – the joint recollection of the lovers and, crucially, the commemoration that Gottfried posits as constitutive of the literary process. Past love is offered like a eucharist for the sustenance of noble hearts, those contemporaries of the author whose sensibility is aroused, sharpened and confirmed by the story of bittersweet passion. Thus the love of Tristan and Isolde does not grow cold, the past is remembered and renewed in the present, death becomes new life. In what, though, does this new life consist? Is it active imitation of the exemplary lovers in one's own affairs? Or is it realized in the contemplative self-immersion of noble hearts in the fictional structures of the literary text? The drift of Gottfried's great macrostructural commentaries runs in the latter direction, toward a renewal of love in the imagination, not in practice. This bold conception of the fictive potential of literature, and its articulation by means of stupendous metaphors, make *Tristan* a landmark in world literature.

Gottfried himself staked a claim to the title of landmark, not in world literature, of course, but in the German literature of his day. In his literary excursus he insinuates his status as laureate in the flourishing tradition of German poetry. That claim was taken seriously in the decades after his death, when authors no longer looked to France for new works to adapt but instead modelled themselves on the now undisputed canon of German classics. Within that canon, Gottfried's was a hallowed name, alongside Hartmann and Wolfram; this status assured his continued reception into the fifteenth century. But classic authors are also apt to be remade in the image of the age that reveres them (indeed that might be a definition of a classic), and Gottfried was no exception. German romance of the later Middle Ages turned away from fictional experimentation to the certainties of history and religion. This development reflected the changing literary taste of the aristocratic public, who wanted romance either to provide historical legitimation for their exclusive lifestyle, or to afford reassurance and escape in politically uncertain times. Gottfried's unconventional celebration of adultery in a royal marriage suited neither of these functions. The story of his becoming a classic is accordingly the story of what aspects of his work later generations chose to accentuate, modify or ignore.

In order to tell this story, we can call on several kinds of evidence: the manuscripts of *Tristan*; references to him by other authors; the works of his continuators and admirers.

Manuscripts

Tristan is preserved in twenty-seven manuscripts and fragments from the thirteenth to fifteenth centuries. This figure represents only a fraction – maybe one tenth – of the total number of copies that must have been made in the same period but have not survived; whether it indicates that Gottfried was less popular than other contemporary classics (Hartmann's *Iwein* is in thirty-two manuscripts, the *Nibelungenlied* in thirty-five, and Wolfram's *Parzival* in eighty) is difficult to say, since the number of extant manucripts is not an entirely reliable guide. Hartmann's *Erec*, the first Arthurian romance in German, is preserved near complete in just one manuscript from the early sixteenth century, yet references and allusions by other writers make clear how well known it was in the thirteenth century. What the manuscripts tell us for certain is that Gottfried continued to attract readers throughout the later Middle Ages, and that these readers were to be found all over the German-speaking world. Although the majority of the manuscripts are from the South West and from Alsace in particular, some are from central and eastern Germany, attesting to a reception far beyond Strassburg. The manuscripts possibly also provide an index of how interest in *Tristan* fell off over time: eleven of them can be dated to the thirteenth century, nine to the fourteenth, and only seven to the fifteenth. If there really was a decline in Gottfried's fortunes, this is to be ascribed to the more conservative taste of later centuries.

The testimony of other authors

Throughout the thirteenth century and into the next Gottfried was revered above all as a consummate stylist. Authors express admiration for 'meister Gotfrit', whose artistry, ingenuity and rhetorical brilliance set a standard they might emulate, but never equal. Their praise often picks up terminology and metaphors used by Gottfried in his literary excursus; by re-using it authors show that they consider him to be in complete possession of the eloquence he had professed to lack. Ulrich von Türheim and Heinrich von Freiberg, the two continuators of Gottfried's unfinished romance, begin with a lament for the golden style that died with the master. Ulrich declares that Gottfried's writing 'is smooth and perfect; there is no poem with diction so glittering as to surpass it in artistry' (ed. Kerth, 11–13); Heinrich regrets the art, eloquence, invention and sagacity that died with Gottfried, who 'decked out this matter in such bright clothes, that I doubt I can think of any eloquence equal to this golden diction' (ed. Bechstein, 23–9). The clothing metaphor is also used by Rudolf von Ems, one of the foremost representatives of the classicizing trend in thirteenth-century German narrative literature. In a literary gallery with clear allusions to Gottfried's own, he exclaims, 'How utterly masterful is his *Tristan*! Whoever has read it can hear without any doubt that he was a tailor of sweet words and a harbour of wise meaning' (*Alexander*, ed. V. Junk, Leipzig, 1928–9, 3158–62). Konrad von Würzburg takes up another of Gottfried's metaphors for good style when he admits, 'Nor do I sit on green clover, moist with the dew of sweet eloquence, upon which master Gottfried of Strassburg sat worthily' (*Die goldene*

Schmiede, ed. E. Schröder, Göttingen, 1926, 94–7). And about a century after Gottfried's death, in 1314, Johann von Würzburg envies the inventiveness that Gottfried had claimed was paralysed: 'Alas dear, illustrious master, bold man of Strassburg, Gottfried a good poet! If only I had your ingenuity' (*Wilhelm von Österreich*, ed. E. Regel, Berlin, 1906, 2062–5).

The continuators Ulrich von Türheim and Heinrich von Freiberg

Twice in the thirteenth century Gottfried's unfinished romance was narrated to its conclusion by another author. The first continuator was Ulrich von Türheim, writing around 1240, the second Heinrich von Freiberg, around 1285–90. Of the eleven 'complete' manuscripts of *Tristan*, nine transmit Gottfried's narrative followed by one or other of these continuations, an indication of how captive medieval readers were to the story-line. The fact that continuations were commissioned is testimony also to the high reputation Gottfried enjoyed in the thirteenth century; his *Tristan* joins those other unfinished narratives by great authors which were completed by another hand. Examples from France are Chrétien's Grail romance *Perceval*, which attracted multiple continuations in the the thirteenth century, and Guillaume de Lorris' *Roman de la Rose*; in Germany Wolfram's epics of *Willehalm* and *Titurel* were accorded the same honour as his great rival (the continuator of *Willehalm* was, ironically, Ulrich von Türheim). It was remarked above that the story of how Gottfried became a classic is the story of what posterity made of him; the continuations of Ulrich and Heinrich provide us with some of our best insights into this process and the milieux in which it took place.

Both continuators wrote for patrons connected with a royal court: Ulrich for Konrad von Winterstetten, one of the most influential men at the Swabian court of the Hohenstaufen kings (he held the offices of imperial cup-bearer and procurator of the Duchy of Swabia, and had been the guardian of Conrad IV and Henry VII), and Heinrich for Reimund von Lichtenberg, a nobleman with close connexions to the court of the Bohemian kings at Prague. Each patron belonged to a literary circle whose tastes were formed by the classics of the 'Blütezeit'; the resemblance between the two circles reveals itself most strikingly in the fact that both of them commissioned continuations or antecedent narratives to the same two works, *Willehalm* and *Tristan*.

The continuations narrate Tristan's marriage to Isolde Whitehand, the love intrigues involving him and his brother-in-law Kaedin, and the lovers' death. Ulrich's source is Eilhart; Heinrich claims to be following the 'Lombard' romance of Thomas of Britain, a puzzling reference which nobody has explained satisfactorily. The episodes highlight the danger for noblemen of falling prey to passion. First, Tristan fails to consummate his marriage out of continuing love for the other Isolde, then Kaedin begins an affair with a married woman, Kassie; her avenging husband kills him and deals Tristan the poisoned wound from which he dies. The continuators treat this material ambivalently. On the one hand they use it to press home the message that the stability of marriage is preferable to uncontrollable passion; on the other they concede that the love of Tristan and Isolde contains an image of the divine love that is symbolized in the marriage sacrament.

Tristan's marriage is presented as a missed opportunity for escape from 'wantonness' and 'folly' (Ulrich, 45–52), the 'sin', 'crime' and 'dishonour' of adultery (Heinrich, 204–16, 269–80). Ulrich thinks that Tristan fails to sleep with his wife because on his wedding-night the first Isolde 'sent the wondrous love-potion as messenger to him' (228–9). Heinrich speculates that just as the light of a heavenly body can be eclipsed for a while, so there may have occurred a temporary eclipse of the potion's force, in the space of which Tristan came to his moral senses and resolved to marry; on his wedding-night, however, the first Isolde's sun dawns again in his heart (217–80, 776–88). For both continuators, the potion represents a stubborn impediment to the full social integration of the hero, and the love it causes is a blot on the escutcheon of an otherwise perfect knight and courtier. Ulrich rounds off his eulogy of the dead hero with the regret, 'If only the love-potion had not led him into folly! It frequently injured his honour' (3581–4), and Heinrich laments, 'Alas! alas! that the love potion once more compelled the lovers Tristan and the fair Isolde' (3005–7). Towards the end of Heinrich's version, Tristan does consummate his marriage, though no explanation is offered for what appears to be a second 'eclipse' of the potion; Heinrich simply reports that Tristan now lives with Isolde Whitehand as a man should with his wife (5962–71). As an event, this has no bearing on the plot, which concerns Kaedin's involvement with Kassie; thematically, though, the evocation of sexual fulfilment in marriage provides a counterpoint to what will be the fatal outcome of Kaedin's coveting another man's wife. The implication is that keeping sexuality within marriage would save all the characters from disaster.

Marriage is an image of Christian love, whose permanence is contrasted by the continuators with the inconstancy of fleshly desire. Ulrich upbraids Lady Love for her fickleness and mutability, and exhorts wise people to avoid her and cleave instead to 'true love, which never perishes' (250–1). This true love, along with 'the love that many a heart desires', sexual love in other words, is commended to Tristan and Isolde Whitehand by her mother when she blesses the couple in their wedding-bed (210–16). Behind her commendation of both kinds of love lies the theology of the marriage sacrament: husband and wife becoming one flesh is a symbol of Christ's loving union with his bride, the church. The superiority of Christian love is preached with still greater explicitness by Heinrich in his epilogue. There he assigns the story its didactic value; calling it a 'mirror' in which all lovers of the world may see the transience of earthly passion, he exhorts every Christian to turn to Christ, 'the true love which is imperishable' (6858–9).

The continuators do not simply hold up Tristan and Isolde as a warning against passion and the flesh; their view of the lovers is also streaked with sympathy. Ulrich pities their suffering and extols their fidelity which, he hopes, will earn them God's grace; it is as though their earthly love might yet bring them within reach of heaven (3631–57). Heinrich similarly evokes pathos in an almost lyrical obituary for Tristan which is punctuated by variations on the statement 'he died for love of Isolde' (6414–80). He also goes much further than Ulrich in suggesting that the lovers' constancy might provide a fleshly image of that true love which never perishes. Like Ulrich (and Eilhart), he recounts how Mark plants a rose and a vine on the lovers' grave; they grow and tangle, visible tokens of the potion's unabated force (6828–41). But in the epilogue, which follows hard upon this episode, the rose and the vine are given a new symbolic value. The flowering rose is Christ; the vine, which Christ caused to sprout from him, signifies Christian believers; the fruit of the vine is human reason, which flourishes thanks to Christ. Believers should incline their hearts and minds to Christ, praying for the rose and the vine to grow together, as they entwined over the noble lovers Tristan and Isolde (6860–90).

The continuators' celebration of the lovers entails a complete reversal of Gottfried. In likening an adulterous liaison to Christian marriage, Gottfried used the religious sacrament as an analogy for earthly love; Ulrich and Heinrich use earthly love as an analogy for religious love. Gottfried is an enthusiast for the 'living paradise planted in the heart' (18066–7); his continuators' sights are set on Christian heaven. For them, heaven is the ultimate goal of everyone: of the lovers, whose devotion may yet bring them to grace; of the king, who enters a monastery to prepare for the next world; of Ulrich, Heinrich and their public, who are included in the prayers that close the poems. This focus on the afterlife provides the clearest measure of how the continuators have stood Gottfried on his head. Gottfried's lovers and his public, the noble hearts whose number includes the author himself, are reunited in a literary afterlife, sustained by the repeated celebration of the eucharist-story. Ulrich and Heinrich hope that they, their public and the lovers will meet again in God's heaven. Where Gottfried uses religious concepts as metaphors for literary creation and communication, the continuators express conventional piety.

Konrad von Würzburg, *Das Herzmœre*

One day, Gottfried narrates, a Welsh harper entertains Mark's court with a lay. Tristan recognizes its theme; it is about 'Gurun and his beloved' (3526–7). Gottfried does not elaborate, but it must be the same as the lay that Thomas' Ysolt sings about Guirun, the lover whose heart was fed to his mistress by her jealous husband (Sneyd[1], 781–90). The motif of the eaten heart is widespread in narrative literature of the Middle Ages; examples of analogues are the *Roman du Castelain de Coucy* and Boccaccio's tale of the lovers Guiscardo and Ghismonda (*Decameron*, IV, 1). But Konrad von Würzburg's version, the *Herzmœre*, is particularly interesting to us because it is told through the prism of Gottfried.

The plot of Konrad's short narrative, written in verse couplets around 1260, is simple. A knight and a lady are devoted lovers. But they are unable to enjoy their love fully because she is married. Her husband discovers the liaison and is determined to put a stop to it. He resolves to make a pilgrimage to Jerusalem, taking his wife along with him, in the hope that she will forget her lover once she is separated from him. The lovers, apprised of the husband's plan, respond with a counter-ruse, intended to save their love. The knight will pre-empt the jealous husband by announcing his own intention of going abroad; by this act he will place himself above suspicion and, when the rumours about him and his lady have ceased, will be able to come back to her. This hoped-for happy end is not to be. Overseas the knight pines for his love and dies of grief, after he has given his squire instructions to cut his heart from his dead body, embalm it and place it in a jewelled golden casket together with the ring that his beloved had given him at their parting. Thus the squire is to return to the lady her lover's heart and her ring. Even this sentimental wish is not to be fulfilled. The husband intercepts the messenger, takes the heart from him, and has it cooked into a dish which he makes his wife eat. When she learns that she has eaten her lover's heart, she declares that she will never eat again. Thus she starves, requiting her lover's death with her own.

The story is framed by a prologue and epilogue. The prologue invokes Gottfried's authority as justification for telling the story: 'I recognize that pure love is no longer cultivated in the world. Therefore knights and ladies should contemplate this story's example, for its theme is unalloyed love. Master Gottfried von Strassburg assures us of this: whoever wants to walk smoothly along the path of true love must indeed hear tales and songs about affairs of the heart which happened long ago to people who exchanged loving glances. There is no denying it: whoever listens to songs or stories of love will be a better lover for it. Therefore I will take pains to make this fine story ring true, so that it can provide an example worthy of love, which should be pure and cleansed of every sort of falsehood' (ed. Schröder, 1–28). The allusions to Gottfried's own prologue and 'Short Discourse' are unmissable: the ideal of love no longer exists in the contemporary world (cf. *Tristan*, 193–7, 12280–2); exemplary stories about lovers from the past are therefore necessary (cf. 12320–5); these stories are a school of virtue (cf. 174–90). All of these points are taken up in the epilogue, which is another collage of sentiments culled from the same passages of *Tristan*. Konrad compares his contemporaries unfavourably with the lovers in the story: 'It is my belief that nowhere was love requited as completely [as by these lovers], nor will it ever be; I can tell this by my contemporaries, for the tie of Lady Love does not constrain them so tightly that they, man and woman, are bound together in such a way that each will suffer the torment of bitter death for the sake of the other. [...] Nowadays [love's] nature has changed, and her rank become so debased that unworthy folk may buy her at a cheap price. For that reason, nobody accepts bodily pain for her sake; nobody holds that in regard any more or esteems what has become the common property of everyone' (534–69). Insufficient devotion, refusal to accept suffering, venality – these are exactly the terms in which Gottfried attacks the lovers of his day and age (cf. *Tristan*, 201–17, 12200–317). Only the noble hearts are exempt, and it is to this group in particular that Konrad also addresses himself. The epilogue closes with an exhortation to them to learn from the story: 'I, Konrad von Würzburg, cannot tell you anything else. Therefore let anyone who intends with a pure heart to do his best willingly take this story into his thoughts, let him learn from it to preserve purity in love. Let no noble heart be daunted! ['kein edel herze sol verzagen!']' (580–8).

The whole of the *Herzmære* – both the story and its frame – is a reduction of Gottfried. It reduces in the literal sense that key themes from *Tristan* (true love is devotion until death; the author's contemporaries rediscover what they lack in stories of exemplary lovers) are repeated in compact and distilled form. It is also a reduction in the further sense that Konrad selects and combines these themes in a way that renders them simpler and starker. His prologue is a good illustration. The individual elements out of which the argument is composed can all be found in Gottfried, but the argument itself – true love no longer exists, therefore we must learn it from exemplary stories – is a reduction of Gottfried's own position. The notion that love stories are a school of virtue is only one of several paradigms in the *Tristan* prologue, and it functions as part of a whole. It modifies what precedes it, and is itself modified by what comes after (above, pp. 53–4). The 'teaching' ('lere') (189) that Gottfried offers turns out not to be a set of precepts to be applied in life by the noble hearts (which is what Konrad envisages), but an experience of love created by hearing or reading literature. The final paradigm of Gottfried's prologue describes this process with a metaphor: the eating of the eucharistic bread, which stands for the noble hearts' self-creation through identification with the bittersweet life and death of the lovers whose memory they recall. This metaphorical eating is reduced to cannibalistic literalness by Konrad. One lover eats the other's heart; this becomes the emblem of the devotion that the epilogue encourages noble hearts to embody in their own lives.

It would be easy to sum up the *Herzmære* as a work that boils Gottfried's subtlety down to literal-minded didactics. Yet to leave it at that would be an inadequate response. Konrad's is an intelligent reduction, which he could not have performed without understanding his model well. He homes in on a crucial question raised by Gottfried, namely: what is the use of old love stories? The answer similarly fastens upon one of the most important claims Gottfried makes on behalf of literature: it has the potential to transform us into better people. Gottfried means this in a far more complex way than Konrad could ever have explained in the brief compass of the *Herzmære*. Nevertheless, the simplicity and starkness of Konrad's question and answer concentrate our minds on the important issues. For we, who come almost eight hundred years after Gottfried, must ask ourselves what we get out of reading his old love story. I have tried to give my answer in this book; it is up to readers, however, to go on finding their own reasons for occupying themselves with Gottfried.

Guide to further reading

Gottfried's *Tristan*: editions, commentaries and translations

The edition of Gottfried's *Tristan* generally used by scholars is that of Friedrich Ranke (Berlin, 1930; fifteenth edition, Dublin and Zurich, 1978). Although he was the foremost scholar of the manuscripts in this century, Ranke never published a complete critical apparatus to accompany his text; for the manuscript variants we must still make do with the earlier and deficient apparatus to the edition by Karl Marold (Leipzig, 1906, revised by Werner Schröder, Berlin, 1969). There are convenient reading-editions of *Tristan* in the original language by Reinhold Bechstein (2 vols., Leipzig, 1869–70; revised by Peter Ganz, Wiesbaden, 1978) and Rüdiger Krohn (3 vols., Stuttgart, 1980). Both of these editions offer substantial linguistic assistance, in the form of footnote glosses (Bechstein/Ganz) or parallel translation into modern German (Krohn); both also deal with problems of textual and literary interpretation in their commentaries and general introduction or afterword. The most extensive commentary is Lambertus Okken, *Kommentar zum Tristan-Roman Gottfrieds von Straßburg*, (3 vols., Amsterdam, 1984–8). The translation of *Tristan* into modern English by A. T. Hatto for the Penguin Classics (Harmondsworth, 1960) remains unsurpassed.

Other primary sources

Editions and translations into English of the romances of Beroul, Eilhart and Thomas:

Beroul, *The Romance of Tristran*, ed. A. Ewert, 2 vols., Oxford, 1939, 1970; trans. Alan S. Fedrick, Harmondsworth, 1970
Eilhart, *Tristrant*, ed. Franz Lichtenstein, Strassburg and London, 1877; trans. J. W. Thomas, Lincoln, Nebraska, 1978
Thomas, *Les fragments du Roman de Tristan*, ed. Bartina H. Wind, Geneva and Paris, 1960; trans. A. T. Hatto (as an appendix to his Gottfried translation)

Readers with a knowledge of French are well served by two recent anthologies of the most important Tristan texts, including the romances of Beroul and Thomas, in the original language and translated into modern French: Philippe Walter and Daniel Lacroix, eds., *Tristan et Iseut: Les poèmes français: La saga norroise* (Paris, 1989); Christiane Marchello-Nizia, ed., *Tristan et Yseut: Les premières versions européennes* (Paris, 1995). The latter contains an edition and translation by Ian Short of the recently discovered Carlisle fragment of Thomas.

The *Tristan* continuation of Ulrich von Türheim has been edited by Thomas Kerth (Tübingen, 1979), that of Heinrich von Freiberg by Reinhold Bechstein (Leipzig, 1877). For the *Herzmœre* see Konrad von Würzburg, *Kleinere Dichtungen*, ed. Edward Schröder, vol. 1 (tenth edition, Dublin and Zurich, 1970); Schröder's text is reproduced, with parallel translation into modern German, in Konrad von Würzburg, *Heinrich von Kempten – Der Welt Lohn – Das Herzmœre*, ed. Heinz Rölleke (Stuttgart, 1968).

Several classical sources featured repeatedly in the discussion of Gottfried:

Cicero, *De oratore*, ed. and trans. E. W. Sutton and H. Rackham, London, 1942

Ovid, *Amores, Medicamina faciei femineae, Ars amatoria, Remedia amoris*, ed. E. J. Kenney, Oxford, 1961; *The Erotic Poems*, trans. P. Green, Harmondsworth, 1982

Quintilian, *Institutio oratoria*, ed. and trans. H. E. Butler, London, 1921–2

Rhetorica ad Herennium, ed. and trans. H. Caplan, London, 1954

Background to Gottfried

For the social, cultural and educational background to German literature of Gottfried's time see:

Joachim Bumke, *Höfische Kultur: Literatur und Gesellschaft im hohen Mittelalter*, Munich, 1986 (translated as *Courtly Culture: Literature and Society in the High Middle Ages*, Berkeley and Oxford, 1991)

D. H. Green, *Medieval Listening and Reading; The Primary Reception of German Literature 800–1300*, Cambridge, 1994

Nigel Palmer, *German Literary Culture in the Twelfth and Thirteenth Centuries*, Oxford, 1993

Max Wehrli, *Literatur im deutschen Mittelalter. Eine poetologische Einführung*, Stuttgart, 1984

The notion of literary fiction, central to my interpretation of *Tristan*, has been much discussed by German medievalists in the last decade thanks to Walter Haug's seminal book, *Literaturtheorie im deutschen*

Mittelalter (second edition, Darmstadt, 1992). Chapter XI analyses Gottfried's prologue and literary excursus. My discussion of *Tristan* has also drawn on the background of canon law, and the theology of marriage and the eucharist; for an introduction to these areas see:

Christopher Brooke, *The Medieval Idea of Marriage*, Oxford, 1989
James A. Brundage, *Law, Sex and Christian Society in Medieval Europe*, Chicago, 1987
Georges Duby, *The Knight, the Lady and the Priest*, Harmondsworth, 1984
Gary Macy, *The Theologies of the Eucharist in the Early Scholastic Period*, Oxford, 1984

The entire medieval Tristan tradition is surveyed concisely by Peter K. Stein, 'Tristan', in Volker Mertens and Ulrich Müller, eds., *Epische Stoffe des Mittelalters* (Stuttgart, 1984). For an up-to-date summary of research on the Celtic origins of the story see W.J. McCann, 'Tristan: The Celtic Material Re-examined', in Adrian Stevens and Roy Wisbey, eds., *Gottfried von Strassburg and the Medieval Tristan Legend* (Cambridge and London, 1990), pp. 19–28. Recent comparative treatments of the story are Gerhard Schindele, *Tristan: Metamorphose und Tradition* (Stuttgart, 1970); Joan M. Ferrante, *The Conflict of Love and Honor: The Medieval Tristan Legend in France, Germany and Italy* (The Hague, 1973); Emmanuèle Baumgartner, *Tristan et Iseut: De la légende aux récits en vers* (Paris, 1987); Merritt R. Blakeslee, *Love's Masks: Identity, Intertextuality and Meaning in the Old French Tristan Poems* (Cambridge, 1989); Alois Wolf, *Gottfried von Straßburg und die Mythe von Tristan und Isolde* (Darmstadt, 1989).

Literary interpretation of Gottfried's *Tristan*

Philologists and literary critics have been writing about *Tristan* since the end of the eighteenth century, and the secondary literature is now voluminous. Everything that has appeared down to 1983 is catalogued in Hans-Hugo Steinhoff, *Bibliographie zu Gottfried von Straßburg* (2 vols., Berlin, 1971, 1986). The bibliography is arranged by theme, so readers can easily find the relevant literature on any specific point or aspect in which they are interested. Work on Gottfried published since 1983 is listed in the regular bibliographical updates provided by the journal *Germanistik*; Okken's commentary and the latest (1991) edition of the commentary volume to Krohn's edition are also good sources of bibliographical information. Because specialist literature in the form of journal articles, contributions to scholarly *Festschriften* and the like can easily be looked up in these bibliographical aids, the following suggestions for further reading are confined in the main to recent books of a general nature.

General introductions to Gottfried:

Michael S. Batts, *Gottfried von Strassburg*, New York, 1971

Christoph Huber, *Gottfried von Straßburg, Tristan und Isolde: Eine Einführung*, Munich and Zurich, 1986

W. T. H. Jackson, *The Anatomy of Love: The 'Tristan' of Gottfried von Strassburg*, New York and London, 1971

Gottfried Weber and Werner Hoffmann, *Gottfried von Straßburg*, fifth edition, Stuttgart, 1981

Alois Wolf, *Gottfried von Straßburg und die Mythe von Tristan und Isolde*, Darmstadt, 1989

Literary histories and manuals with chapters or articles on Gottfried:

Karl Bertau, *Deutsche Literatur im europäischen Mittelalter*, Munich, 1972–3

Horst Brunner, ed., *Interpretationen: Mittelhochdeutsche Romane und Heldenepen*, Stuttgart, 1993 (L. P. Johnson)

Ursula Liebertz-Grün, ed., *Aus der Mündlichkeit in die Schriftlichkeit*, Reinbek, 1988 (Horst Wenzel)

Kurt Ruh, *Höfische Epik des Mittelalters*, vol. 2, Berlin, 1980 (see also Bertau's response to Ruh in his *Über Literaturgeschichte*, Munich, 1983)

Kurt Ruh, ed., *Die deutsche Literatur des Mittelalters: Verfasserlexikon*, 2nd edition, vol. 3, Berlin, 1981 (Hugo Kuhn)

Studies of a specific theme or aspect that also offer a general interpretation of the work:

Winfried Christ, *Rhetorik und Roman: Untersuchungen zu Gottfrieds von Straßburg 'Tristan und Isolde'*, Meisenheim, 1977

Ingrid Hahn, *Raum und Landschaft in Gottfrieds Tristan: Ein Beitrag zur Werkdeutung*, Munich, 1963

C. Stephen Jaeger, *Medieval Humanism in Gottfried von Strassburg's Tristan und Isolde*, Heidelberg, 1977

Dietmar Mieth, *Dichtung, Glaube und Moral: Studien zur Begründung einer narrativen Ethik mit einer Interpretation zum Tristanroman Gottfrieds von Straßburg*, Mainz, 1976

Rüdiger Schnell, *Suche nach Wahrheit: Gottfrieds 'Tristan und Isold' als erkenntniskritischer Roman*, Tübingen, 1992

Petrus W. Tax, *Wort, Sinnbild, Zahl im Tristanroman*, second edition, Berlin, 1971

Tomas Tomasek, *Die Utopie im 'Tristan' Gottfrieds von Straßburg*, Tübingen, 1985

Franziska Wessel, *Probleme der Metaphorik und der Minnemetaphorik in Gottfrieds von Straßburg 'Tristan und Isolde'*, Munich, 1984

Anthologies of critical essays:

Rainer Gruenter, *Tristan-Studien*, ed. W. Adam, Heidelberg, 1993 (brings together important essays first published by the author in the 1950s and 1960s)

Paola Schulze-Belli and Michael Dallapiazza, eds., *Il romanzo di Tristano*, Trieste, 1990 (recent essays, in German and Italian, mostly on Gottfried)

Adrian Stevens and Roy Wisbey, eds., *Gottfried von Strassburg and the Medieval Tristan Legend*, Cambridge and London, 1990 (recent essays on all aspects of Gottfried by British and North American scholars)

Alois Wolf, ed., *Gottfried von Straßburg*, Darmstadt, 1973 (an anthology of the most influential essays written between 1925 and 1969; many of them have become classics of Gottfried scholarship)

After Gottfried

On German literature in the later Middle Ages, see Joachim Heinzle, *Wandlungen und Neuansätze im 13. Jahrhundert* (Königstein, 1984) and Thomas Cramer, *Geschichte der deutschen Literatur im späten Mittelalter* (Munich, 1990). Heinzle discusses Gottfried's continuators and Konrad von Würzburg, and gives references to further literature.

The critical fortunes of *Tristan* in modern times have been traced in several studies: Rosemary Picozzi, *A History of Tristan Scholarship* (Bern and Frankfurt, 1971); Reiner Dietz, *Der 'Tristan' Gottfrieds von Straßburg: Probleme der Forschung (1902–70)* (Göppingen, 1974); Beatrice Margaretha Langmeier, *Forschungsbericht zu Gottfrieds von Strassburg 'Tristan' mit besonderer Berücksichtigung der Stoff- und Motivgeschichte für die Zeit von 1759–1925* (Zurich, 1978); Waltraud Frisch-Rößler, *Der 'Tristan' Gottfrieds von Straßburg in der deutschen Literaturgeschichtsschreibung (1768–1985)* (Frankfurt, 1989).